THE ART OF
EXCELLENT
PRODUCTS

Enchanting Customers
with Premium
Brand Experiences

RICCARDO ILLY

HarperCollins
LEADERSHIP

AN IMPRINT OF HarperCollins

© 2022 by Riccardo Illy

All rights reserved. No portion of this book may be reproduced, stored in a retrieval system, or transmitted in any form or by any means—electronic, mechanical, photocopy, recording, scanning, or other—except for brief quotations in critical reviews or articles, without the prior written permission of the publisher.

Published by HarperCollins Leadership, an imprint of HarperCollins Focus LLC.

Any internet addresses, phone numbers, or company or product information printed in this book are offered as a resource and are not intended in any way to be or to imply an endorsement by HarperCollins Leadership, nor does HarperCollins Leadership vouch for the existence, content, or services of these sites, phone numbers, companies, or products beyond the life of this book.

ISBN 978-1-4002-2511-8 (eBook)
ISBN 978-1-4002-2510-1 (TP)

Library of Congress Control Number: 2021949876

Printed in the United States of America
22 23 24 25 26 LSC 10 9 8 7 6 5 4 3 2 1

To my wife, Rossana,
and my daughter, Daria

CONTENTS

INTRODUCTION

I have lived my whole life in Trieste, in what is now Italy. Our city is not famous in the way that Venice is, or Capri, or Rome. We sit on the easternmost corner of the Italian border, a short drive from Croatia and a little to the west of Slovenia. Our culture, the food, and the local dialect are shaped by our neighbors and by our history as a seafaring people.

We Triestini see ourselves as sailors: the sea is as much a part of the city as the land. In the summer, we sail and swim and fish. In the winter, the Bora wind brings cold air down from the mountains and across the Karst Plateau, behind the city, churning the harbor, throwing up white waves, and chilling the air. Our main square, the largest seafront square in Europe, opens onto the Adriatic Sea. This reflects how closely our fortunes are tied to the water (sometimes literally, when those winter storms flood the piazza).

Trieste is in Italy, but it is not completely Italian. At various points in our history, we have been claimed by Rome, the Germanic Lombards, and the Franks. Napoleon occupied us three times. We were proclaimed a free city by the Holy Roman Empire in the fourteenth century and were under the protection of Austria until November 4, 1918, when we were liberated by the Italian army, only to return to being a "stateless city" (like Monte Carlo) after World War II. The Iron Curtain was just six miles from the center of our city. Finally, in 1954, we returned to Italy, and we have been happy to consider ourselves Italian ever since. (However, our region, Friuli Venezia Giulia, is one of five autonomous regions in Italy that have greater power over their own legislation and administration, due to diverse cultures and three distinct languages.) Most Triestini carry this collective memory of our cultural rootlessness. It's made us more adventurous and bolder than we might have been otherwise. We take care to preserve our varied past with religious and cultural associations that allow old traditions and knowledge to survive. All the while, the fortunes of our city have ebbed and flowed with the vagaries of history and the ever-changing populations of immigrants who have made their mark on our home.

Trieste is a place that lends itself to beauty. I couldn't live anywhere else. We are known as "Vienna on the Sea" because of our graceful neoclassical architecture and the many statues that remind us of the Habsburg Monarchy. Our streets bustle with cafés where patrons enjoy midafternoon espresso and cappuccino that only in Trieste are served in the same typical small espresso cup. This café culture was adopted from the Austrians (along with their appreciation for Doric columns and intricate plasterwork figurines that decorate the interiors of the cafés). There is a special quality of light: maybe it is the Bora, scrubbing the air of pollution, or the way the light reflects off the plateau that sits behind us like an amphitheater. Either way, Trieste is beloved by photographers and artists. It is beloved by writers as well: James Joyce wrote parts of *Ulysses* here.

My grandfather chose this city to start his business because it was already busy with coffee and café culture. He realized our port gave us access to the world. But most of all, he loved the experience of living here, as do I. Like him, and like most Triestini, I drive to the mountains on most winter weekends to ski. In the summer, we sail. We see one another in the theaters and operas or in restaurants that line the piazza, eating food pulled fresh from the Adriatic and the mountains and flavored by our history: Austrian omelet, Greek lamb, Hungarian goulash, Slovenian *jota* (hotpot).

I often wonder if we could have done what we did with illy anywhere else. Probably not.

There are other reasons, besides the simple pleasures of life, that we can operate so effectively here, rather than decamping to a larger center of industry. For one, Trieste has a highly educated population that has access to a large, state-subsidized university. Unlike other secondary and tertiary cities, our young people stay here, even when bigger opportunities beckon from Milan, Rome, London, Tokyo, or New York. Why? Because the quality of life is too good to risk losing. We are a civilized place, a town that offers art, science, commerce, and nature, while also taking care of our citizens with great schools and health care.

This balance between the necessities of modern business and the necessities of a well-lived life is key to our success. The sea has connected us with the global business community. Our culture prioritizes beauty, art, nature, and science. These priorities have allowed us to develop a passion for quality, a desire always to excel, and a determination to leave our world improved rather than degraded. We call these fundamental beliefs *Incanto,* and they are the foundation of everything we do. illy is a business: we wish to grow and profit and succeed. But we are also woven deeply into our community. Our choices and our actions reverberate through our town and our larger network of global suppliers, sales accounts, and subsidiary companies. Our work is not just for us, it is also for them. Every facet of our business, be it our products, our management, or our employees (many of them members of the same multigenerational families) must be in service of a sustainable future. And this future must be one that focuses on quality and on lasting for generations, supporting our grandchildren and their grandchildren.

DEEP ROOTS, TALL TREES

Like their contemporary descendants, the Romans were obsessed with quality. They painted elaborate frescoes and set exquisitely detailed mosaics in the floors of their villas. They drank good wine and pressed olives for oil. They mastered a concrete so strong that their buildings survive today (though the technology to mix the concrete has been forgotten). When I ride my motorbike to the office, I pass by the Roman theater. It was built in the first century CE, and though it is weathered and the original facades and walls are long gone, we still use the stage and the amphitheater for occasional concerts and performances. It feels natural to sit on the stone benches under a warm summer sky and enjoy music or a play, just as our very distant ancestors did. I doubt the original inhabitants of Tergestum, as the Romans originally named Trieste, imagined the rock concerts that occasionally play here. However, I'm sure, in one way or another, they assumed that their distant descendants would still use and enjoy their theater. This belief that some of what we do is not for ourselves but for the people we will never know, decades or centuries or millennia from now, is key to everything about the Italian way of business.

Some of this belief system is born in the nature of the products that we grow and produce in Italy. In Italy there are families that have managed their vineyards for more than six hundred years. A new vine must grow for five years before it will produce a grape. The wine must wait five more years before we can sell it as Brunello di Montalcino. On our estate, Mastrojanni, we grow olive trees and press the olives for oil. Some of these trees are a thousand years old; the quality is still excellent. So, in Italy, we are used to building an environment that will create consistent, exceptional quality for generations. We understand that we may not be doing this for us.

When we expand our operations at illy and consider new investments and acquisitions, I focus less on whether it will enhance my own life and more on the belief that someone will benefit from it. Those "someones" might be my own descendants, or those of the many families who work for us, or even the descendants of farmers on the other side of the world who support their families by selling raw materials to us.

THE THREE LEVELS OF QUALITY

When you understand the Italian love of quality and commit to it as the primary philosophy for running your business, you are committing to consistently generating a product that surprises and delights your customers. Why? Because to connect with discerning consumers, you have to offer them something *more*, something charming and unexpected. We break quality down to three levels.

First, you have the company that makes a product that offers *necessary quality*. These are the sweaters that may itch but keep you warm. The food that doesn't taste so good, but that nonetheless satiates your hunger. The car that isn't comfortable but gets you where you wish to go.

Then there is the company that offers products of *expected quality*. These are the sweaters that are both warm and soft. The food that is both tasty and nutritious. The cars that are both comfortable and reliable.

And finally, we have companies that offer products of *augmented quality*. These are the sweaters that are warm, comfortable, and delightful. The food that is tasty, nutritious, and surprising. The cars that are efficient, pleasant, and unexpected.

This concept of augmented quality, and specifically the idea of surprise, is a cornerstone of everything we do. It is one that drives businesses in Italy to global success, even in dire economic times. Think of a fashion brand like Prada or Ferragamo. The anticipation for a new season is electric; how will they interpret the cultural moment in a way that surprises the intellect and delights the eye?

This is the essence of augmented quality: a garment made by Prada uses exceptional material and impeccable manufacturing techniques. However, that's not why fashion aficionados gravitate to Prada's garments or sacrifice to buy them. After all, serviceable cashmere sweaters are available in mainstream brands everywhere. What makes Prada's dresses, coats, and suits so desirable is that mysterious extra, the sense of surprise and delight that comes from small, carefully considered details, the superlative nature of the raw materials, and the assurance that the customer is buying something that is, in its nature, superior to all competitors.

This delight, this surprise, is essential to everything we do. There is a reason our espresso cups are mounted on saucers that elevate the cup, showcasing it like a work of art. There is a reason we often commission actual works of art to decorate those same cups. Our customers know our coffee will be excellent. If we wish to continually surprise them, to offer them that augmented quality, we must enhance their purchases in ways they do not expect.

THE FOUR PILLARS OF INCANTO

So, how do you offer augmented quality? Through the years, I have identified four fundamental philosophies of Italian businesses. I call this family of philosophies Incanto. It is something unique to Italians, born out of our eye for beauty and our desire for simple, elegant quality.

In this book, we will look at some quintessentially Italian businesses that embody the Four Pillars of Incanto:

* A perception of absolute superiority by consumers, in other words, perfection
* A unique supply chain, incompatible with that of mass-market producers
* The best materials available
* A deep and broad attention to the issues of social, environmental, and economic sustainability

All of these elements are equally essential to creating a business that can produce consistent quality in successive generations, while adding to the well-being of the community in which it is based. When you look at your business through the lens of Incanto, you will inevitably see new possibilities and new avenues for your own initiatives.

After all, when a new business isn't going to be making a profit for decades, you are forced to have a long-term perspective. Incanto gives us a framework to do this. Looking at a quarterly report doesn't make sense in a winery. Even five years is too short a period to assess how you are doing.

Instead, you have to look at other elements of your business. They may be less easy to read than a column of figures, but they are equally important. When I assess the health of my businesses, I look at the figures that are available, but I also review less tangible assets: I talk to my customers to see if my product is still enchanting and surprising them. Am I able to source the very best coffee or cacao beans, and are my relationships with these growers still happy and friendly?

I look at the scores that my wines are earning in various guides and read the feedback from customers. Am I making a product that is worth talking about on social media? Are our goods being tagged in positive ways? I talk to my employees: Are the older workers still encouraging their children to work at illy? And finally, I will look at the impact my company is having on the environment. Are we doing everything we can to maintain the good health of the land that grows our crops? Are we an asset or a liability to the people who live around our factories?

These four elements are crucial to an Incanto business: a superior product, a unique supply chain, the very best raw materials, and a commitment to sustainability. If you can hold on to these core principles and accept that you may have to work more slowly than your competitors, then you can build a radically resilient business. It may take many years, but it's okay because you realize that growth needs constancy. Rather than chase immediate returns, you build a foundation that is rooted both in your family and in the larger community.

Let's break these down further:

- When we discuss absolute quality, we are talking about the value as perceived by the consumer.
- When we say to develop a supply chain that is not compatible with mass production, we are actually

discussing rarity. By definition, mass production is the common condition; rarity is when you can only do things in limited quantities.

- The use of hard-to-access raw materials creates a condition that makes it hard to imitate, because it's hard to acquire the raw materials.
- Finally, the attention to sustainability creates the organization that makes it possible to take advantage of this.

INCANTO IN AMERICA

I understand that this is not a business model that is traditionally embraced in America. Often, when I talk to my contemporaries in New York, San Francisco, or Miami, I hear the intense pressure they are under to deliver shareholder value, dividends, and so on. They share how they are required to find ever cheaper raw materials, explore ways to lower employee costs, reduce benefits, cut the prices of their products to the bone, and find creative ways to circumvent environmental protections. In the very worst-case scenarios, private equity investors acquire legacy companies (perhaps one like my own), break them apart into different assets, and sell them to other parties. These assets may be the factories the companies have owned for generations, which they must now rent back, delivering this income to the new owners, and destroying the health of a solvent company overnight. It is astonishing to me how many great American companies, often originally family owned, have been run into the ground by this kind of short-term thinking.

I am here to propose a different way of doing things, and, fortuitously, I believe we are at a moment in history where this kind of radical change is possible. Like America, Italy was hit hard by the fallout of the global pandemic of 2020. It has forced illy to consider every facet of our business and reconsider what we must do to make our company more viable, more sustainable, and more desirable moving forward. Two of our chief raw materials are cacao and coffee beans. So, what happens to our suppliers as the temperate band, suitable for growing both crops, moves ever farther from the equator? Our employees are our engine. They have a deep and irreplaceable body of knowledge about our operations. So, how do we keep them safe and ensure they remain as invested in the success of our company as we are? Most important, how do we continue to offer the high level of consistent quality that our customers expect from us, and hold on to our clientele, even as the economy struggles around us?

Our answer to these questions is Incanto. We believe that when times are difficult, it becomes more important to maintain a high-quality product, even when those around you may be looking for ways to cut costs at every corner. Likewise, it is critical to invest in the health and longevity of your supply chain. Consider the families living in remote parts of the world who grow or produce the materials you require for your product: Are they still surviving and thriving? Do they have the resources to adapt to a changing climate, and are you assisting them to the best of your ability?

Throughout this book, we will tell the story of Incanto from three perspectives. The first is practical: How do you create a business that prioritizes quality, insists on sustainability, and always strives to produce a better product while being profitable? The second perspective is intellectual: What are the elements of Incanto, and how does each affect the quality of your product as well as the quality of life of the people who enjoy it and those who produce it? And the final question is philosophical: How can Incanto improve the health, happiness, and long-term prospects of people all over the world?

THE NEW GLOBAL WEALTH

Our business truly is global: we have seen an explosion in our customer base in the past ten to twenty years. My grandfather marketed chiefly to Italians, my father also to Europeans and Americans; now we have new customers who live in mainland China, Brazil, Russia, Thailand, India, Korea, and so on. These newly wealthy people (China alone has 5.5 million millionaires) have, for the first time in their lives, real choice. They have the financial resources to buy what they want, travel wherever they wish, and enjoy the best quality available to them. Wealth is relative, so we define it less by numbers than by this ability to make choices and pick priorities. It is the classic hierarchy of needs: when a person is warm, fed, safe, loved, and accomplished, they can focus on those experiences that lead to a sense of self-actualization, or that make life worth living. Companies like ours, and perhaps like yours, have an opportunity to create products that, simply put, add to the joy of life.

There is a contradiction here. As a company we have always embraced sustainability, for both practical and philosophical reasons. Yet, often, when people first become wealthy, their instinct is to buy more: another car, multiple wardrobes. Perhaps they want the rarest of materials, leading to the depletion of already vulnerable wildlife. Perhaps they buy more food than they can possibly eat. However, our goal is to persuade our customers to buy *better.* You can only drive one car at a time or eat a certain amount of food. So, make those items the very best you can afford.

As we tour Italy in the next hundred-plus pages, you'll see how different companies have devised ways to give their customers an experience of Incanto. Some do this by replacing quantity with extraordinarily rare (but sustainably harvested) materials. Others replace signifiers of extreme cost with their opposite: centuries-old techniques forgotten by their competitors. At illy, we believe in *indizio*, meaning "clue" or "sign." We use it to describe how a higher price is not normally sufficient to say if an item is of superior quality. So, for our fellow professionals, and our new customers (and anyone else who wishes to join), we have created the Istituto Internazionale Chocolier (the International Institute of Chocolate). The courses are professional level, but designed to be engaging for, and enjoyed by, anyone with a passion and a love for chocolate. Similarly, we have the illy University of Coffee, where anyone with a passion for coffee can learn all the details about how we create a superlative product.

Our "universities" give our customers a chance to educate themselves, improve their knowledge, and enjoy the everyday delights of an exceptional glass of wine or coffee, or a piece of chocolate, with a more thoughtful, sophisticated appreciation. Even more important, once a customer sees the immense amount of work that goes into growing, harvesting, fermenting (yes, both coffee and cacao beans must be fermented before they are processed), refining, and forming the chocolate, the price of the chocolate makes sense. They no longer resist spending a little more because they feel a sense of appreciation for all the work that has gone into it.

Just as wealth is not necessarily about money, so quality is not necessarily about cost. Instead, quality is about conveying a message of something *better* to your customer. I truly believe that the simplest experiences in life can be superlative, full of joy, and worthy of celebration: a perfectly brewed espresso,

served in the midafternoon for a few euros can be as delightful, and as surprising, as the most expensive meal in the finest
quality restaurant.

FAMILIA

There is another facet to Incanto, which we have touched
briefly on already, that is key to our philosophy. Our business,
and all the businesses featured in this book, are family-owned
and (in most cases) -managed enterprises. Many, like illy, are
multigenerational. Some have been controlled by the same
family for hundreds of years. This can be complicated! When
families work together, the drama and petty disputes of the
breakfast table can follow them into their business. So, we take
great care to ensure that employees do not supervise their
close relatives, and ideally that close relatives do not work
within the same departments. What is important isn't so much
that multiple generations of the same family are involved in
the day-to-day running of a business. Instead, what is important is that the people who own, operate, or manage a business
adopt the mindset of a family. How would I define this?

The first element is a blend of loyalty, values, and culture.
At illy, we are loyal to our employees, and they to us. I am
committed to the people who work for me. I understand that
without seasoned, experienced employees who understand
both the logistics and the spirit of our business, we will not
succeed. In return, we treat our employees well. The people
who work at all levels of illy encourage their children to work
for us. They have pride in being a member of the illy family.
In a sense, their families and ours are united.

The second is a sense of continuity. I do not feel the pressure that a nonfamily-owned business might of generating

record profits overnight or slashing costs to increase share-holder dividends. My priority is always the longevity of the company and the fundamental strength of what we do and how we do it. When I plant a new vineyard, I know it is un-likely to make me richer or enhance my life in any way. In fact, it is more likely to be a significant investment that requires my energy and more money over time. However, it will add to the long-term stability and strength of illy, even if I am not here to see the day it goes from red to black. Really, this should be the core mission of every company, private or public, big or small.

Here's another benefit of the family-run business: it allows you to step outside of what you might learn at an MBA program and avoid problems that established business protocols can't plan for. From a business-school perspective, the rules are established and logical. Of course a successful business listens to its customers; of course it invests in the newest technologies. But sometimes, focusing solely on the logical rules can leave you unprepared for Black Swan events (an unpredictable event with potentially severe consequences). You are so certain that you are fully prepared for all eventualities that you are vulnerable to the unexpected. Years ago, two planes, one commercial, one private, collided over the Amazon. One had been flying at the wrong altitude, resulting in a near-head-on collision. However, the crash was also partly due to the nature of the modern navigation system. Both aircraft were flying within just a few feet of the flight path when they collided. An older, imperfect navigation system, one that depended on fallible humans rather than precise artificial intelligence, would have given them a better chance of avoiding disaster since no human navigator could have gotten a plane exactly on the precise route. Likewise, family-run businesses are inherently more "human" in nature. We make decisions based on preferences, personal philosophies, and deep-rooted instincts. This can certainly cause problems, but I believe it also allows us to be more flexible, adaptable, and open to the unexpected.

Finally, a family-owned business is a joyful thing. There is a sense of comradery and collaboration. You are all in this thing together. I like to say that you can't make beautiful things fearfully. You must approach the challenge of business with ferocious, unbridled joy. And you must live joyfully too. Working with my family is full of this sense of profound, purposeful joy. But if you aren't in a family business, what can you do to bring this sense of passion, delight, and shared vision to your company?

THE JOY OF AN INCANTO BUSINESS

I am lucky that my business is based in a country where these elements seem essential. We are surrounded by customers who reward exceptional products and thoughtful design. (One unusual problem we have had is customers who cannot bring themselves to throw away the illy coffee tin, but accumulate so many empty tins that they stop buying coffee, fearing they will have nowhere to store them.) Our customers are willing to pay a higher price for a reliably delightful experience. I am sure that many readers will initially think that these concepts cannot translate to their own business, that their customers will never accept a higher price or a longer wait. I disagree. My experience, first at illy and then at our other brands, including Domori chocolate, Mastrojanni wine, and Agrimontana jam, has taught me a simple truth: a company that makes a promise of quality to its customers and keeps that promise over the years, even when it is sometimes difficult to do so, will retain those customers. Why? Because they trust us to deliver the same product, reliably, year after year. While other brands slowly degrade their quality in the name of enhanced profits and shareholder satisfaction, we are in the unique position of being answerable only to ourselves and keeping that promise of quality, come what may.

Over the course of this book, we will explore the eleven key elements of Incanto: Perfection, Coherence, Beauty, Authenticity, Family, Simplicity, Cultivation, Refinement, Relationships, Patience, and Surprise. For you, the reader, we will look at ways you can learn from the Italian philosophy of Incanto. It will not be possible for you to retroactively rebuild your company as an Italian-style, family-run business. However, it is possible to adopt an Italian mindset, one that prioritizes quality over short-term profits, and sustainability over environmental degradation. illy has weathered many storms. We have had years when our future was not guaranteed. We have had to make incredibly hard choices; for instance, reducing our products to just one line of coffee. However, every choice we have made has pointed us in one direction, toward our long-term survival. Because, as CEO, I make decisions that will only pay off years down the road, I am in a position to plan our company's future for generations to come. Because of this, the illy brand is as resilient to the vagaries of the global marketplace as it is possible to be.

I hope that you will find ideas within this book that you, too, can adopt to your business, to propel you into a more stable, sustainable, and multigenerational future.

ONE

PERFECTION

Perfection is the first of the Four Pillars of Incanto. Without perfection, you will never offer your customers something so sublime, so surprising, so delightful, and so unexpected that they will forever seek out your product above all others. When I describe the quality of perfection to my students, I use the word *joy*. A moment or product of perfection brings joy, tempered by the sometimes bittersweet awareness of perfection's transience. One knows that perfection arrives seldom and that it will soon depart, so try to prolong the joy for as long as possible.

I find it useful to remember that utterly flawless perfection is nearly always beyond the reach of human beings. Instead, we use the concept of perfection as a goal or a target to aim for, so we can perform at our very best. Likewise, we encourage our customers to view perfection as something to continually search for. The very act of seeking out perfection inevitably improves the experience of life by helping you to develop a more discerning taste and a more refined eye while rejecting superficial experiences or substandard items that ultimately add little to the joy of living. Many artistic traditions—be they medieval illuminated manuscripts, Navajo rugs, or Japanese *wabi sabi* pottery—push this idea further by deliberately introducing small flaws in the belief that "only God is perfect." Of course, for most of us, the flaws, no matter how subtle and imperceptible, will already be there.

Striving for perfection may sound elitist. The products and experiences that we generally consider "perfect" are often expensive and hard to access or acquire. Securing a table at Harry's Piccolo in Trieste, Eleven Madison Park in New York City, or La Tour d'Argent in Paris is an endeavor. It helps to have elevated social connections, unlisted phone numbers, and of course enough money that settling the eventual bill causes you no sense of undue distress. I thoroughly enjoy a meal good enough to have earned a few Michelin stars. However, the idea that perfection is the preserve of the very wealthy, or that it must be obscure or hard to find, is anathema to the philosophy of Incanto. Every summer, my wife and I retreat to the mountain resort of Alta Badia for a few weeks of relaxation. We will often spend an afternoon searching for mushrooms among the larches and firs of the forest of the alpine Dolomites. I am not a great expert in fungi. However, between the two of us, we have sufficient expertise and confidence to pick enough edible chanterelles or porcini to make a meal of risotto or an omelet, avoid poisoning ourselves, and enjoy a pleasant morning on the slopes of Piz la Villa. I consider this experience, and the eventual meal, as perfect as any elegant and refined dinner. Both surprise the imagination and delight the senses, albeit for very different reasons.

EXPERIENCING PERFECTION

Perfection is a quality that can be appreciated and understood by the nonprofessional. Just as I do not need to be a mycologist to appreciate both the hunt for, and the taste of, the local mushrooms, you do not need to be a sommelier to enjoy an excellent glass of Barolo. Likewise, a casual observer need not be an architect to see that Palladian villas, such as those that dot the city of Vicenza, are pleasing to the eye, and that their elegant simplicity reflects a happy marriage of form and function.

One of my favorite works of art is *La Gioconda,* better known in America as the *Mona Lisa.* If you are a serious art historian, you understand that the portrait is one of the first examples of a technique called sfumato, whereby da Vinci did away with the bold outlines and delineations of earlier Renaissance paintings. Instead, he used multiple layers of translucent oil color, applied one thin layer at a time over months, to build up an ethereal, glowing portrait filled with a strikingly timeless ambiguity. Yet you don't need to be an art expert to understand that da Vinci's enigmatic portrait is a masterpiece. There is simply no discussion. No formal education in art history is required to see this.

At the same time, *La Gioconda* is perennially surrounded by tourists who are unable to fully immerse themselves in the experience of this piece of art. The painting is barricaded from the Louvre's crowds by a semicircular bannister and a large wooden table. It is smaller than you might expect, and locked behind glass that inevitably dulls her appearance. You are lucky if you can get within twenty feet of the painting. One must wait upward of three hours to enter the crowded room, and the guards move you on before you've even had a chance to catch your breath and look at her. There is no possibility to lose yourself in the beauty before you or absorb the details of da Vinci's masterpiece.

The tourists are in the presence of perfection but are disconnected from it by the scrum of people, desperately trying to get a photo to prove they were there. Often, they neglect the thousands of other astonishing artworks in the museum and leave directly after viewing *La Gioconda*. Why? Because these novice art lovers have been taught to believe that viewing *La Gioconda* means something in a way that viewing *The Raft of the Medusa* or *Une Odalisque* might not. They are confident that they have picked the right work of art to experience (however superficially) and be elevated by, and that they will be correct in sharing their appreciation of it when they get home.

There are two disconnects to consider here. The first is the idea of perfection that cannot be fully appreciated. This is something that you as a product designer or business owner must consider. As we learn from *La Gioconda*, it is not enough to create perfection. First, you must also create an environment that allows the viewer or customer to experience it. The second is education: How are you teaching your customer to understand and appreciate the perfection of your product and recognize its superiority over your rivals?

As you consider your products and the way your consumer relates to what you sell, it's also imperative to understand the different qualities of perfection. On the one hand, perfection can be a brief and ephemeral experience: that glass of Barolo, or perhaps a moment in the natural world where you fully feel the joy of life. On the other, it can be a durable consumer good of superlative quality and design. That Prada jacket we mentioned in the introduction? It would be challenging to find a flaw. The cut is exquisite, reflecting current fashion while also suggesting future trends. The tailoring slims the figure and flatters the wearer. The silkiness of the lining allows the wearer to put it on and take it off without an awkward struggle. The jacket, just like that ephemeral moment in the natural world, adds joy to one's life. In this case, partly by subtracting the obstacles and frustrations that a less perfect item would add to it.

Brief ephemeral moments as well as long-lasting and durable products give you an opportunity. If the latter is beyond your scope, perhaps due to the nature of your product, then focus on the former, and find ways to create an experience that is charming, surprising, and memorable.

WHY PERFECTION MATTERS

Before we move on, let's consider what happens when perfection is not a priority. For a "soft" product, like our jacket, it merely disappoints. The sublime thrill of an unexpected detail, perhaps a delicately hand-worked buttonhole, is not there. Your customers might never be able to fully articulate why the jacket was ultimately not worth the outlay. But they will move on to another designer, leaving your garment unworn at the back of their closet.

I experienced this myself as a young man, when I worked and saved all summer, even selling my beloved motorbike, to buy a Fiat 127. I drove it out of the lot, quite happy, even if I could already sense that something was not quite right about the manual gearshift. When I drove it back, I was dismissed by the service department. They said I was too young, too new a driver to understand how a car should work. Eventually the car fell out of warranty, and almost immediately needed a new gear box. For the next forty years, I drove German cars. Recently, Fiat reinvested in its car division. It is once again prioritizing quality, and I now own a Panda 4x4 for the mountains. Still, Fiat missed out on forty years of my business, because it did not prioritize perfection, or take my teenage self seriously, or consider it worth nurturing and holding onto me as a customer.

In a "hard" product such as technology, medicine, or transportation, imperfection can be deadly. A good example is the ongoing debacle at the American aviation company Boeing. After decades as a much-loved and much-trusted company, they have had two major issues with both their workhorse, the 737, and their new flagship, the 787. The former was hastily reworked with larger engines and software to compensate for the shift in the aircraft's weight and balance. The software, overly complex and difficult to use, caused two deadly crashes. In the 787's case, a new factory complex in Charlotte, North Carolina, started turning out 787s with so many flaws and such shoddy workmanship that one airline, Qatar,[1] allegedly refused to accept aircraft manufactured there.[2] I doubt that any internal reviews cited a "lack of perfection" as the problem. But looking at it through an Incanto lens, we can see that Boeing lost sight of the importance of constantly striving for perfection. It was willing to take shortcuts in its design process, pushed employees to the point that they were forced to cut corners or were so aggrieved they no longer cared about their work, and delivered an end product that numerous Boeing executives knew was problematic. The end result: 346 deaths in the 737 Max, temporarily grounded 787s, thousands of jobs in peril, billions of dollars lost, and an irreparable fracture of public trust.

As we will discuss in coming chapters, one goal of Incanto is also sustainability, which is another way Boeing has fallen down. I regard sustainability as primarily an environmental consideration. However, it can also refer to creating a company culture that is resilient to unexpected pressures and stresses. I believe Boeing made a grave mistake by allowing its highly educated and irreplaceable workforce to lose trust in the company. Boeing, like other deep-rooted, decades-old businesses, has a tremendous amount of goodwill within its workforce and the larger consumer community. It is so well loved that aviation enthusiasts from around the world journey to Everett, Washington, to tour the factory or watch aircraft take off on test flights. It is an astonishing mistake to squander that.

DOES YOUR CUSTOMER CARE?

One common criticism of prioritizing perfection is that your customers simply do not expect or even want it. This is less an issue in Italy, but it *is* something I see regularly in America, where imperfection, be it disastrous as at Boeing, or more banal as in the burned coffee served at numerous nationwide coffee chains, is more accepted. If your customers aren't demanding perfection, it may simply be because they have never had the chance to experience perfection. They might not realize that their coffee is bitter, because the beans have been purposefully over-roasted to compensate for the poor quality of the raw ingredients or to create a uniform taste that can be easily replicated in thousands of cafés. Likewise, you may also experience numerous forces from within your organization, pushing you to prioritize speed, lower costs, enhance worker productivity, or increase shareholder value. My rebuttal to this argument is always the same: at some point, one of your competitors will figure out how to offer a dramatically better version of what you do.

Another issue is businesses that think they do not need to offer a product with that key quality of Incanto: surprising, delighting, perfection. Think of a time in your life when you made some small purchase, expecting very little, and were surprised by the quality of the experience. Perhaps you stopped alongside a highway for a quick lunch, expecting generic food, poorly presented. And yet, as you ate, you realized that the cook had fully planned and executed a simple meal with passion and conviction. Instead of forgettable, it is delicious. The ingredients may be the same as another diner down the street, yet that person, laboring in the kitchen, felt inspired to go beyond the minimum required. You will of course seek out the same restaurant, and the same experience, every time you return to the area. Now imagine the same thing happening in your field: What happens to your business once your rival figures out a way to offer an elevated product?

PERFECTION IN ACTION: BIASETTO

Just 120 miles from Trieste is a business that embraces the same ideals of using the best possible ingredients, a passion for surprising, unexpected results, *and* a workforce that is united behind a vision of superior quality. The business is a bakery called Pasticceria Biasetto, and within its *laboratorio* (the Italian term for a professional kitchen), it creates superlative pastina, so good that I consider it among the finest in Italy.

Biasetto is based in Padua, a small city west of Venice in Italy's northern region. Shakespeare set *The Taming of the Shrew* in Padua,[3] but today the city is better known for its university, one of the oldest in Europe; and for its Basilica del Santo (also known as the Basilica of St. Anthony). I travel there often, sometimes with university students, sometimes in my capacity as an illy executive (Biasetto uses a wide range of illy products, including Domori chocolate, Dammann Frères tea, Taittinger wine, and Agrimontana jams).

TELLING THE STORY OF PERFECTION

A visit to Biasetto begins with a quick coffee (illy, of course) in the bright café, decorated in bold colors and modern, large-scale prints that glow in the afternoon sun. Chef Luigi is always quick to offer a pastry. Often, I pick the macarons. Now, Biasetto's macarons are different from how you might imagine. A traditional display of macarons is full of vivid colors: a neon pink for the raspberry, a deep purple for a fig or plum, blood red for cherry or pomegranate, and a bold, intense green for pistachio. At Biasetto, the colors are slightly muted, more subtle. The hazelnut, chocolate, and coffee are all similar shades of nut brown; the pinks are demure, the greens a light pastel. When new customers walk in, they may initially think that the macarons are a little plain. However, just as our novice art enthusiast should be educated about the lesser known works in the Louvre, so Biasetto's customers are educated about the quality of Luigi's products. As he explains: "We take our creations directly to the mouths of the customers. And any word that can be said before the tasting experience, to explain and present, becomes secondary after. Because it is the taste, the harmony of taste, the textures, the flavor, the length, all these elements become the judge."

Behind the counter, waiters playing the role of brand ambassador patiently explain that the pastries are natural, that there are no artificial colors or flavors, and that only the very best ingredients are used. They offer a small sample if necessary. Just as with *La Gioconda*, the quality quickly becomes apparent, and the customer is won over.

Luigi was raised in a family business, albeit not Biasetto. His father was a shoemaker and, like his son, demanded perfection from himself. Luigi tells me that his father had simple tools, yet the shoes he made looked as though they were produced in the most equipped atelier. As he speaks, he grows emotional. For Luigi, as for any truly passionate innovator, his love for his work runs deep. He tells me more about his father, a man who shined his shoes with care that was obsessive. "There is no doubt that growing up, in childhood, I would hear words that influenced me, so at the age of three or five or eight, or ten, hearing about perfectionism and witnessing an attitude and behavior that strived for perfection, that certainly shaped my way of thinking."

Every time I visit Biasetto, I am reminded that perfection requires buy-in from everyone involved: your employees have to love the work and the product as much as you do. Like all the businesses discussed in this book, Biasetto is a family business with a strong founder culture. Luigi is consumed with his passion for his business, and his love and belief are infectious. That passion can be a double-edged sword. As Luigi explains: "The touch of the expert hand makes all the difference. So, this search for perfection, for the craftsman, for those who aspire to perfection, is essential. It is a way of thinking and living."

Like Luigi, I struggle to understand people who don't bring a deep and passionate love for their work. Perhaps his attitude is understandable when one works for a big company, lost among the ranks of employees. But in a small business, each action is critical. Workers must be invested in the belief that their work matters, and that every choice to either try their best or, as Americans call it, "phone it in" affects the business in an immediate and critical way.

"I have a hard time dealing with those who work in a superficial way, without care," Luigi told me. "There is always a need for a chain of control, a hierarchical system. I have no doubt about this. I should point out that the craftsman, the one who pursues the idea of perfection, is never happy, never.

And it is difficult to live with a person who is never happy. Our quest for quality is a sort of fundamentalism, a positive one that aspires to a never-ending perfection.

"So, we have to find other fundamentalists. I need to know not only my producers, but their family, their *fazenda* [the chocolate estates], where they live, who their parents are, and how their children grow up, so that I can have an idea of what their mindset is, what they will aspire to do when they grow up.

"I often tell the HR [human resources] manager that a candidate should come to the interview with his or her grandmother; only then can I understand more. I don't care about parents; the grandparents are more revealing. It is difficult to do so, but some grandmothers have come to the job interviews. So, I think with them you understand the story, where one comes from."

Luigi's observation asks an interesting question to any business owner, especially one who is creating a product of exceptional quality: Do you know what the guiding principles are of the people who work for you, and do you understand the influences that shaped them as they grew up? What kind of questions are you asking them, and what kind of shared influences and ideals feel crucial to you? Here is an opportunity for you to emulate a key ingredient in the Italian love of perfection: finding people who share your vision. It may sound whimsical to ask to meet a prospective employee's grandmother. In America, where so few people live with their grandparents, it might not be that revealing anyway. However, you can adapt this concept to your own interviewing process. Dig a little deeper and understand the person sitting across from you beyond the superficial details of their résumé.

Luigi is not demanding a certain standard of education or references. What he wants to know is whether that individual is capable of understanding what an obsession for perfection actually entails. Did they watch as their parents or grandparents labored over something until it was perfect, as Luigi did? If not, it's unlikely that the prospective employee will ever understand why Luigi labors himself. Later, Luigi shared that he generally prefers to hire people at the beginning of their career, rather than midcareer, as they are more receptive to his passion for perfection and willing to continually learn. Your demands might be different. But by learning who your potential employee is as a person, rather than simply a worker, you have a better hope of finding someone receptive to your ideals.

THE HEART OF PERFECTION

Perfection can have strange origins. At Biasetto, the beginning of most products is a strange creature called the *mother yeast*. The mother is an amorphous blob, pale in color and strong in apple-cider-vinegar smell. She sits in a large plastic bin, sheltered under a linen cloth, in a warm corner of the kitchen. The mother (in America, she would be called a sourdough starter) is almost certainly the least expensive ingredient that Biasetto uses. Yet she is the most valuable and irreplaceable. Biasetto's mother's origins are unclear: no one is completely sure where she came from, but she is at least ninety years old. Several years ago, Biasetto registered her with the Puratos Center for Bread Flavor, the world's only sourdough library near Brussels, created in an effort to preserve diverse yeast strains from around the world (similar in concept to the Norwegian Svalbard seed vault).[4]

Luigi can always order more flour, chocolate, coffee, or jam. It would be a more complicated story to replace his starter, which has been cultivated slowly over decades, every passing year deepening the flavor as the strains of yeast grow more complex. At night a technician takes a small piece of the mother, feeds it water and flour, and places her into a separate plastic container, this time roping it tightly shut. Why? Because as the mother feeds off of the flour, she grows with an astonishing power: at her peak, the mother yeast can push ten times her weight. She is quite simply a force of nature.

Like all Incanto businesses, Luigi understands the importance of sourcing the very best raw materials. Yet at the heart of his business is a simple ingredient made out of flour and water and time. She requires care, understanding, and experience to survive. There is an important lesson here for any business: perfection has to be a priority at the very root of your work. You cannot build a perfect house on a poorly laid foundation. Luigi's "foundation," the starter, is nurtured and tended like a firstborn child. Let's draw another lesson from this: the very best raw materials are not always about cost or scarcity. Sometimes they are about superb but simple ingredients, plus a deep, passionate, almost obsessive understanding of the mechanics of your product.

The mother yeast is finicky, demanding, and prone to dramatic displays of bubbling anger when her needs are not met. Luigi's competitors have found easier ways to make their dough. Large industrial bakers use liquid natural yeast that lasts about a month with little care. It comes in a bottle and is relatively stable. Some of Luigi's more artisanal competitors keep their yeast alive in water, where it thrives without as much supervision as the mother. These more commercial, standardized ways of baking are easier and more predictable. No one is losing sleep or fretting over the health of the starter. Their building has a reliable, predictable foundation. However, the house itself might lack character, charm, or surprise.

The mother lives and breathes. Luigi explains: "If I receive a piece of a mother yeast from a colleague and bring it here, the next day it has a different identity than that of the colleague's original. Through the mother yeast, the idea of quality is transferred to the product. And this is why the mother yeast must be educated in an orderly manner. I talk about 'education,' because in the case of mother yeast, it is born and reborn every time it is kneaded, it is transmitted, it is transferred, it carries our identity, the aromas and the texture."

Perhaps Luigi's life would be easier if he used industrial yeasts. Right now, tending to the mother is a huge part of his job: Luigi knows to the smallest decimal point how the mother's ever-changing pH balance will affect his pastries and bread. His most famous product, the panettone,[5] requires a pH of 4.2. Earlier this year, he had to discard more than 880 pounds of dough because the bakers who prepared it misread the numbers noted on a board above the mother. The acidity was off, and though it's quite possible his customers would not have noticed the change in flavor, Luigi immediately discarded the batch.

I doubt that Pasticceria Biasetto's customers understand how crucial the mother yeast is, or how much she affects the taste, texture, and overall quality of the products they buy from Biasetto. What they do know is that the breads, pastries, and cakes they buy from Biasetto have something special: the texture and specifically the elasticity. The perfection that permeates every element of Biasetto begins with the mother.

So, first, perfection starts at the very first step of your business. For Luigi, it is the yeast that causes the chemical and biological processes essential to baking. Second, perfection requires that your employees understand the process, accept that it is critical, and set aside all other considerations to ensure this standard is maintained. Third, cheap and superficially appealing flourishes, like using artificial colors or flavors that might give a quick hit of sugar or strong taste, are rejected, even when life might be simpler if you used them. Fourth, your employees understand the nuances of the story and can share it with existing and potential customers.

I chose to write about the mother yeast because she is a keystone element of seeking perfection in business. If she fails, so does everything else. She is temperamental and finicky. An employee who does not particularly care about her could do irreparable harm by adding chlorinated water, overheating her, or feeding her the wrong mixture of flour. The mother has a tangible value: she is the root of all the baked goods Biasetto makes.

Yet, she also has another role. I'd argue that the mother and the care she requires set a tone for the way Luigi runs his business. His employees understand that every facet of what they do requires this level of attention. By giving so much attention to her care, he has created a culture of focusing on details. It is inherent in everything they do. Employees who can't or won't understand this will quickly realize it is not the right job for them.

Seeking perfection is exhausting. There is a cost. One cannot pursue perfection without a complete dedication to attaining it, and that dedication can take everything from you.

As Luigi points out: "Something strange I witnessed is that once my father decided to close the business [as a shoemaker] about ten years ago, he hasn't touched a pair of shoes ever since. He just had had enough—he was so tired, exhausted. Now, I don't know if I could do it. But maybe the pursuit of quality runs you out at some point.

"As a parallel, I think about art. If you are not careful as an artist, it can devour you. Many artists are also remembered for their madness, devoured by an exhaustive search for a color, an idea, a form. For us, it is a search for perfection on taste, on presentation. So, sometimes I tell myself, you need to accept that not everyone can get there, you need to accept the limits of others, because otherwise you live poorly."

THERE IS A PRICE TO PAY FOR DEMANDING THE BEST

As you consider how to pursue perfection in your own company, consider:

- What element of your business is the keystone of perfection? If you can't identify the keystone, then dedicate some time to thinking it over and identifying which element of your work is so foundational that nothing can go right without it.
- Are you ensuring that your employees feel as personally invested in the pursuit of perfection? If the answer is "no," what can you do to improve this?
- Is your passion for your business and your product in balance with the need to have quality of life? There is little benefit to perfection at work if your home life is unhappy. This is especially relevant if you are hoping to create a multigenerational family business.
- Finally: Are you telling your customers a story about your product that features the sublime, unexpected, superlative nature of what you do?

T W O

COHERENCE

erhaps you are wondering why I chose the word *coherence* as an important element in an Incanto business. After all, *logical, rational,* or *predictable* are all terms that convey similar meanings that could be used to define a series of actions or goals that a business can adhere to in order to succeed. I use *coherence* because the term suggests an ethos or spirit: it's a way to live one's life as well as a strategy to organize one's business. For instance, coherence is a kind of guide in my life, both in business and in my leisure time. I believe in simple things, executed perfectly. illy is founded on this principle. Every decision we make reflects it. It's the same with my personal life. My family lives in a simple but beautiful house in a village on the plateau surrounding Trieste, from where we can see the sea. We don't believe in certain social conventions: I married in blue jeans and sneakers; my wife wore blue jeans as well. I never wear a tie and prefer to avoid the places where one is required. Nonetheless, we both wear nice clothes of the finest quality.

My choices, from how I dress to how I live, mirror the way I approach illy. From the moment I wake, my actions and thoughts are in alignment. Every step I take, no matter how seemingly inconsequential, points in the same direction. This may seem irrelevant, but it is a form of what is called *vertical coherence*. It's when your short-term goals align with your long-term goals, and your long-term goals align with the overall story you wish your life (or business) to tell. This is crucial for your personal ambitions in life and business when you are an employee. It is doubly important when you are in senior management and are setting the tone for an entire organization.

Likewise, *horizontal coherence* is equally important. This means that the stuff of your life—the car you drive, the food you buy, the environment of your office, the preference for recyclable glass over disposable plastic in a factory canteen—reflects the fundamental beliefs of your life. Everything is coherent. Everything tells the same story. In France they have an expression, "*noblesse oblige.*" This means that nobles are obliged to behave well and coherently. Their home, clothes, food, and behavior must be appropriate to their status.

I understand that in many businesses there is barely the time or resources to execute the day's actions, let alone worry about an overarching vision like this. You may be understaffed. You may have had multiple positions consolidated into one job that completely consumes the lucky employee's life. The pressure to make compromises here or shortcuts there may mean that your actions throughout the day are completely incoherent. Creating a coherent structure can initially feel quite traumatic. In the next few pages, you'll read about the drastic steps we had to take at illy Group to bring our products into alignment with one another. However, without coherence, the power of your brand is diluted to the point that your employees may feel confused and adrift, and your products are indistinguishable from your competitors'.

In chapter 4, "Authenticity," we will talk about the importance of authenticity and creating a story about the heritage and history of your brand. These two kinds of coherence, vertical and horizontal, are critical for this. Italians treasure authentic brands because we are reassured by their consistency over the years. We trust the products we buy because our grandparents trusted them. This personal connection is what guides us to pick a box of pasta from a shelf or select a shoemaker. This trust requires consistency and coherence. When you prioritize coherence both in space and time, you are codifying this storytelling.

- *Vertical* coherence means to be consistent in your actions over the years.
- *Horizontal* coherence means all your different daily actions are in alignment with each other.

The payoff for coherency is long-term survival. If your business is a "pop-up," then coherency might not be necessary. Your customers know you will not be around in six months, so they are not invested in your long-term vision. But if you are building a company with a long-term perspective, then it is critical you stay coherent and build trust from your first day of operations onward.

THE SMALL AND COHERENT BUSINESSES OF ITALY

I believe that smaller Italian companies are uniquely coherent in the world. After the devastation of World War II, Italy boomed, partly due to the Marshall Plan. Our young, rural population largely relocated to big northern manufacturing cities like Turin, Milan, and Padua. These new arrivals held onto their love of simple but perfect pleasures of the country: fresh olive oil, handworked leather goods, home-cured meats, and simple but well-made clothing. They quickly found existing small businesses selling the foods and goods they wanted. New brands also sprang up to supply these goods. Today these companies, such as the tie-maker E. Marinella, the shoemaker René Caovilla, and aperitif distillers like Braulio or Cocco, are tightly focused on the quality of their goods and maintaining the supply chain necessary to produce them.

These companies sell superb goods, yet you almost certainly have not heard of them. They sell in their own stores or limit distribution to the immediate area, and they do not focus on marketing or advertising. Why not? First, these companies are family run. They have been creating the same product and telling the same story about that product for two or three or ten generations. Their businesses are profitable, but not so profitable that they can easily invest in expensive campaigns, expand into new markets, or develop new products. Instead, they focus on being consistent and coherent; they rely on existing customers recommending their products to their children and grandchildren.

It is possible to take companies like these and expand them. However, the danger lies in losing that sense of coherence and that unified understanding of who you are, what you do, and why you do it. These local businesses survive because Italians still prefer quality. They know that if they do one thing very, very well, for multiple generations, they will retain their reputation for quality and develop a name for themselves. Opportunities for these small companies to grow are not exploited. Instead, the families remain in one spot, stay small, but survive for decades and eventually centuries.

Conversely, American businesses often struggle because of a fundamental misunderstanding of a company's function. They believe that rapid growth is more important than a coherent ethos. They don't take the time to build trust with their customer, or when they do they are quick to sacrifice that trust when an opportunity to downgrade services or raise prices presents itself. Companies such as Uber use strategies like surge pricing or classifying drivers as "independent contractors" to maximize profits at the expense of workers and customers. Instead of building a culture of trust, they create a situation where some parties feel abused by and distrustful of the app.

A satisfied customer is a loyal long-term consumer. He will buy the existing and new products of the company and will spread its knowledge to more and more consumers. Likewise, a happy employee is a long-term employee who will develop invaluable knowledge about the business and use her experience and insight to keep the company stable and healthy.

ANOTHER WAY TO CONSIDER COHERENCE

When I describe the concept of coherence to my students, I often fall back on another of my great loves: music. First, think of a discordant, unpleasant piece of music. It is physically painful to listen to. The music lacks elegance; no two elements fully work together. Conversely, classical music is not only pleasant to listen to, it also fires nerve cells in the cerebral cortex, triggering the part of the brain that handles the higher functions of reasoning and thought. Gustav Mahler, among the first classical composers who might be considered "modern," is a favorite of mine, specifically his Symphony no. 9. However, no matter which piece of his music you pick, it works as part of the overall story of who Mahler was, the world in which he lived, and how he observed and reacted to that world.

More recently, the composer Philip Glass has spent his career exploring harmonic tonality and the power of repeating the same musical structures over and over again. Completely different from Mahler, yet equally effective. Despite their differences, they are both profoundly coherent. You can pick two pieces from any point in these two men's careers and see a relationship between them. My goal with my businesses is similar: I wish that my customer can pick any two products, from any of our businesses, put them side by side, and see a coherence between them. If customers know that they love the quality of our coffee, they will be equally confident in our wine or chocolate. Why? Because all our brands reflect the same "short recipe" philosophy of minimal ingredients and maximum quality. Our customers trust us to deliver a consistent experience across every product.

There are consumers who are not interested in our products. Someone who dislikes our chocolate and prefers a sweeter taste or novelty flavors will most likely not be interested in any of the brands. They will not prioritize the same things we do. And this is okay. Part of coherence is being unambiguous about who you are and what you stand for. And an inevitable element of this is that what you stand for will not please everyone.

WHEN COHERENCE FALLS APART

On August 14, 2018, the Morandi Bridge, a suspension bridge that sailed high above a residential district in Genoa, collapsed.[1] Forty-three people died and six hundred were suddenly without a home. It was a deeply shocking moment, similar in effect to the September 11, 2001, attacks in America. My coworkers and I gathered around a TV screen, utterly horrified. The bridge, built in the late 1960s, had been made of concrete, something we Italians have been proud of since the Roman era. To see it crumble like that was viscerally painful. It felt like a personal failure for every Italian watching. Even more shocking, the bridge was managed by a subsidiary of one of the most trusted names in Italian manufacturing: Benetton.[2]

If you were young and fashionable anytime between 1967 and 2000, you most likely wore Benetton.[3] Their sweaters were bold and bright, and the colors and patterns coordinated across an entire outfit. In the 1980s, Milanese teenagers adopted *paninaro* style (named after the sandwiches they loved to eat), wearing Benetton, Fiorucci, and other designers as a way of rejecting the turbulent and overtly political 1970s. Billboards all over the world showcased Oliviero Toscani's images of interracial and same-sex couples; an activist dying of AIDS; a newborn, unwashed baby, complete with umbilical cord. For decades, Benetton dominated European fashion: the styles were bold, the marketing was provocative, and the franchised mono-brand business model was effective.

However, Benetton struggled with the rise of fast fashion. Though it pioneered the idea of lightning-fast capsule collections in the 1980s, it was still slow compared to Zara or H&M. Benetton's quality was higher, pricing out the new population of bargain shoppers looking for a weekly wardrobe update. A factory was destroyed and hundreds of employees died in the collapse of the Rana Plaza commercial building in Dhaka in 2013. The company expanded in other slightly questionable and incoherent ways, including a business deal involving indigenous lands in Argentina that some felt was disrespectful to the native people.

By the early 2000s, Benetton was no longer telling a coherent story about what it was and what it might mean to its customers. It no longer prioritized its signature sweaters. Worse, the brand had built its identity around thoughtful provocation, pushing people to be more tolerant and open-minded. Yet it had diversified in a way that was inconsistent with what "Benetton" meant. Through its construction division, the family had control of more than two thousand miles of toll roads. Alas, it was no longer making many sweaters, something Luciano Benetton acknowledged was like "taking the water out of an aqueduct"[4] for its core brand. If Benetton had worried less about expanding into unrelated (though lucrative) side ventures and focused more on meeting the challenge that Zara posed, perhaps it would still be the uniform of young and aspirational people all over the world.

COHERENCE REQUIRES SACRIFICE

When I first started working at illy in 1977, we had a problem similar to the one Benetton is facing: the company had lost touch with the founder's vision. illy had multiple blends and lines of coffee, all reasonably successful and popular. However, this was not our grandfather's dream. He had wanted to make the very best coffee in the world because he believed that people would always seek out the best and be willing to spend more to have it. Nonetheless, by the late 1970s, only one, "The Speciality," was coherent with that strategy and pointing in the right direction of simple perfection. The Speciality (now known simply as illy coffee) accounted for less than half of our sales, yet it was clear to us that illy needed to focus on one superb product rather than a dozen good ones.

Unlike the small businesses I just described, my family had the resources and ambition to grow into a national and then international brand. When I decided to get rid of all the blends except The Speciality, I put myself in the shoes of potential customers. Why should they buy coffee from a company hundreds or thousands of miles away? The answer was obvious. Our customers would only buy our coffee if it offered quality that the local roasters couldn't provide. The other couple of dozen illy blends were similar to the ones that local roasters could offer, but The Speciality was unique; nobody else was able to match it.

We believed focus was critical because serving different blends with different tastes to different customers prevented us from identifying the brand with the concept of quality.[5] By offering "something for everyone," such as a blend for each hotel, restaurant, or café we were serving, we were not moving coherently in the direction we wanted to go: a strong brand with a reputation for impeccable quality. My first proposal as a salesperson was to stop production on all coffee blends, except for The Speciality, 100 percent Arabica, and to completely discontinue our tea. Arabica coffee cost about twice as much as our competitors' blends. According to our strategy, we needed to offer the best coffee in the world, priced higher than most of our competitors.

This was not a particularly popular choice. As in many family businesses, a lot of my immediate relatives relied on a regular income from the company. My decision to potentially halve our revenues overnight seemed risky, and I felt the responsibility of suggesting this solution. However, my instincts told me that illy was an incoherent company, representing nothing much to our customers, and in danger of being over-taken by a more distinctive brand. By reducing our product line to the one truly essential item, we began to tell a more coherent story about who we were. Equally important, our employees understood what illy stood for: simple, consistent perfection. Today we sell twenty times the coffee we did in the 1970s, with one product rather than about twenty.

Here's the interesting twist: my long-term goal was to di-versify and grow our company bigger (we eventually began this process of diversification in the early 2000s), but we first had to retract, shedding every product that wasn't in align-ment with our idea about what illy deserved to be. I knew that illy could become a fully global brand, but to do so it had to stand for something. Our grandfather's dream had been to produce the best coffee in the world; at the very beginning, in 1933, he also produced chocolate with the same qualitative objective and ran a farm where he planted fruit trees to later produce his jams. World War II forced him to abandon both products. After the war, he continued with coffee only.

This is an idea that you can incorporate into your own strategy. What does your company stand for? What is your promise to your customers? For us, it is always to offer the very best product in each sector. For you, it could be a differ-ent value—perhaps reliability, innovation, charm, or prod-ucts that are considered "classics" and won't fall out of fashion. The next thing to consider is, "Does every decision I make, both in my own life and as a decision-maker at my business, point in the same direction?" If the answer is "no," then you may have to consider shedding the elements of your business that are detracting from that core, coherent prom-ise. Once you have simplified your products (or your way of doing business) down to the point that everything is coherent both vertically and horizontally, you can begin to expand in a more logical and systematic way.

COHERENT PRICING

Here is another way you can use the power of coherence to put your brand ahead of less coherent brands. Most Incanto businesses try to keep their pricing uniform across all distribution channels. Generally, a quality-conscious customer is willing to pay a price that feels appropriate for the product in question (at least more willing than a customer who is primarily motivated by price). However, if that quality-conscious customer gets consumed by looking for that Incanto product at a slightly lower price, perhaps online or in another store, he or she can be distracted from the original goal of simply purchasing the product.

Incanto businesses purposefully avoid this by keeping prices stable across all channels. It may mean not being available for purchase on large and popular websites, or avoiding third-party sales as much as possible. The key element is simply to avoid the "race to the bottom" in which so many brands find themselves trapped. So, if your product is of superior quality, avoid promoting by price. This strategy inevitably defocuses the customers' attention away from your primary selling proposition: the quality of the product and your promise of coherency and consistency. If your product is being sold in an independently owned store, then your "story" or the image of your product is almost entirely in the hands of that shop owner (one reason illy will not always supply branding materials such as signs to businesses that do not exemplify our standards and ethos).

Finally, it is far easier to convince a customer that your product is of high quality if the price is also high. It is far harder to persuade your customer that your product is of high quality when the price is too low. This strategy does not work if your product is a commodity or if it is more service oriented. So, pick the strategy that aligns most closely with the nature of your business.

In chapter 5, "Family," you'll read about how freezing weather in Brazil decimated the coffee plantations that supply our beans. We were forced to pay far more for the Arabica beans we rely on. In fact, the prices more than doubled. We couldn't absorb this increase, so we had to increase the prices. Even when the green coffee production grew again and the price stabilized, we didn't reduce the price to what it had been. Instead, we kept the price static to avoid having to increase it again and again in the future. Instead of fluctuating as costs changed, we increased the price once, and then we remained stable for a long time. When your product is of an elevated quality, it is always better to keep a consistent, dependable price rather than a price that is erratic and unpredictable.

DOMORI AND COHERENT EXPANSION

Consistent, coherent pricing will help as you expand across broader markets too. All our products are of such refined quality that their prices are in alignment with one another. It simply wouldn't make sense to add a brand to our stable at a radically different price point. In the late 1990s, I was looking for another piece of my grandfather's vision: a "short recipe" chocolatier whose product reflects the illy ethos and could round out our brand family. Short recipe is an idea integral to everything we do. It is literally what it sounds like. Any product we make must have the absolute minimum number of ingredients possible. Our jams are fruit and sugar. Our wine has no additives. Our teas are whole leaf, with no risk of contamination. And now that we were looking for a chocolate company, I was adamant that any company we bought had to reflect illy's values: it must be short recipe, offer complete control over the supply chain, have the simplest possible production methods, include a commitment to sustainability, and use raw materials that were so fine they could be processed at lower temperatures, preserving quality.

It was also important that the company be family owned and managed so it would share our outlook for slow, responsible growth and maintaining quality above all else. We found this was Domori, a small company founded by a young economist, Gianluca Franzoni, who was passionately committed to resurrecting the Criollo cacao bean in Venezuela. We bought Domori, keeping Gianluca on as the chairman of the company. In accordance with the illy ethos, we were determined to maintain the unique way of processing cacao that Gianluca Franzoni had implemented. We maintained the simplified supply chain and production, reinforcing the joint venture with cacao growers in Venezuela and replicating it in Ecuador to grow the extra-fine Criollo beans exclusively for us. Our production line was perfected to reflect the quality of the ingredients: because they are of such superior quality, we can roast them at a temperature 20 percent lower than our competitors. Likewise, we use a proprietary machine to conch them (essentially a form of refining) for shorter periods and lower temperatures.

Here is the interesting thing about using these extraordinarily rare and high-grade beans: generally, lesser species of cacao, like the Forastero bean, are roasted at a high temperature to get rid of the bad flavors and the volatile acidity typical of this cacao. However, this constant process of refining and conching at high temperatures also gets rid of the *good* flavors. At the end of the refining process, the chocolate has almost no flavor at all. The final step is to add in flavorings and other elements to make the chocolate palatable. You may think that I am describing low-grade chocolate that you'd buy for a child. In fact, even well-known brands that you would recognize on American supermarket shelves as "better quality" European chocolates use these methods. Our strategy is to buy the very best raw materials and preserve quality rather than eliminate and replace defects. If we used a commodity, we wouldn't care so much about the process, because we wouldn't have that much quality to preserve in the first place. However, since we are starting from a place of quality, every step of every process is framed around preserving quality, flavor, and texture rather than hiding bad elements or adding new ones.

There is an important lesson here for any business that is determined to create an Incanto level of quality:

All the various elements, like raw materials, supply chain, and sustainability, are essential. However, your process, and especially what you do in the final step, is where you can make the biggest leap from average to distinctive, or Incanto quality. Conversely, the final step is also where you can destroy the superior qualities of your raw materials if you handle them incorrectly.

Our process allows us to preserve the very best flavors of the chocolate. Most chocolatiers are not interested in our low-impact process, but it is worth it for us. We boil our jam in a vacuum chamber in order to boil it at a cooler temperature of 140 degrees Fahrenheit rather than 210. Most jam makers, however, boil their jam at atmospheric pressure.

Again, since they aren't using the best quality fruit, they don't think it matters. Their flavors aren't good enough to preserve them the way we do.

To create coherence in a business, you first of all need to clearly identify your mission (who you want to be in the market) and strategy (how you want to achieve your objectives). Everything we make is a combination of the best raw materials and the best refining processes. Our production is coherent across the board, as are our products.

The final task is to find and fix the incoherent elements. Domori methods are fundamentally incompatible with the methods that these large chocolate makers use. Our methods can't eliminate the "off" flavors of the Forastero cacao. Likewise, if our competitors used the Criollo cacao beans, they would ruin it with their process, which is not designed to keep the best flavors. Remember what I said about vertical coherence? Our short-term goals for Domori are in line with our long-term goals: to create a family of products that share a coherent ethos and that together tell a compelling story about illy Group. But it is important to remember that these bigger brands are also coherent businesses. Just because they have different goals from illy does not mean that there is anything fundamentally wrong with what they do or how they do it. They are simply working toward a different vision of a coherent company.

It is impossible to mix the philosophies of an Incanto business like Domori with a mass-market business. Likewise, it would be pointless to try and run one of our subsidiaries in a way that was fundamentally out of alignment with the illy ethos. If we were willing to compromise or to make radical changes to our production methods, we could perhaps grow Domori faster. Instead, we have gone in the opposite direction, creating our own internal technology to process the beans.

In 2011, Domori decided to expand into professional chocolate for pastry chefs and gelato makers. We designed and built a brand-new production line to produce a professional chocolate with "Domori's style" (high concentration of flavors) and the technical requirements (for example, fluidity, necessary for incorporating chocolate into baked goods) for the pastry chefs. When the new line was finished, the quality of the chocolate was excellent, but the fluidity was too low; after working for weeks with the machine's supplier, we couldn't find a solution other than to add a new ingredient to increase the fluidity. But this decision would conflict with Domori's short-recipe policy. After deciding to engage an engineering student who had written his thesis on the problem, we finally found the solution. Instead of a single ten-cylinder refiner, he suggested we use two refiners with two cylinders; the fluidity increased at the level of the best competitors, maintaining the higher concentration of flavors.

Coherence isn't always the easiest path (even though it is quite literally the straightest, always heading forward toward the same goal). For illy, coherence has been essential because it gives me one absolutely inviolable rule to guide all our actions. I know that everything I do must point toward the highest possible short-recipe quality. That is always the first consideration in any decision. I challenge you to define your own inviolable rule of coherence. What is the very first question you must answer when you consider any move in your company? And what must the answer be? Once you have determined this question and this answer, make it clear to every employee, from your cleaning staff to the top of the managerial hierarchy.

THREE

BEAUTY

A love of design and beauty is built into the DNA of every Italian. The Romans decorated their villas with mosaics whose intricate colors and patterns, perhaps a duck with a perfectly iridescent green neck or a rabbit whose eye gleams mischievously as it steals away a bunch of grapes, are still marvelous to see. This duck's feathers still shine, and the rabbit's audacity charms, though the artist and subject are both long dead, as indeed is the entire civilization. For me, beauty is harmony. It's the way colors merge together, creating a mood that speaks more clearly than prose. A beauty like this can also be emotional. The waterfront of Trieste faces due west, and every evening the sunset illuminates the city with a rose-red and gold aura that reflects off the water and the buildings, painting the city with a magical wash of light. Experiencing this is profound. One feels a complex love and connection to a place that simply cannot be put into words. I like to think of beauty like this as the salt of life. Without it, we still exist, but we will not experience the extremes of either joy or sadness that a fully lived life must contain.

I think there is a reason Italian designers and businesses prioritize beauty and have made beautifully designed, emotionally resonant, and visually pleasing products a priority. We live in a country that is itself simply beautiful. It encompasses the rugged crags of the Dolomites, rising above verdant valleys; soft-edged foothills covered by vineyards; graceful flat lands crossed by rivers like the Po and the Tiber (Italian: Tevere); and our rugged and rocky coasts, broken by small sandy beaches, covered in neatly ordered rows of bright beach umbrellas. The wild and rocky Aeolian archipelago— too small for many tourists, too far from the big cities for most Italians—completes the beauty of our country. Perhaps we demand beauty in the products we buy because we are used to being surrounded by it in nature. Or maybe our commitment to creating beautiful goods, from furniture to clothes to objects to cars, is a kind of gratitude to Mother Nature for having given us such gifts. You can understand the passion of the Italians for beauty just by looking at how they dress, at their houses, and their cars or motorcycles.

Beauty, or the lack of it, can be a deal-breaker for Italians. For instance, as much as I love to walk in the mountains or along the coast, I won't wear Birkenstocks. True, the shoes are very comfortable. They are easy to take off when you reach the water, or layer with socks when the weather gets cold at altitude. One can easily wear the same pair in nearly any climate. And yet they are so ugly that I can't persuade myself to buy a pair, even when (as occasionally happens) they become temporarily fashionable, and all the chic young people of Paris or New York are suddenly wearing them. These shoes are rarely seen on Italians, no matter the global fashion trends.

There are some people, and some organizations, whose sensitivity for beauty is very low. The distribution of this sensitivity is like a bell curve: In the center you find the majority of individuals or businesses with an average level of sensitivity to beauty and aesthetics. At the sides are the extremes, some with a much lower or higher sensitivity for beauty. The fact that they don't care about beauty doesn't mean they are not committed to other technical aspects. Birkenstock sandals are very comfortable, made with the best materials, and assembled perfectly. They are just ugly, at least to my eye.

Here's another element of beauty: it is subjective. It takes a point of view to prioritize beauty. By emphasizing something so personal, you can risk alienating potential customers, even as you strengthen a link with customers whose tastes reflect yours. For this reason, family-run Italian businesses are well positioned to have a defined point of view about what is beautiful. They are small enough, yet established enough, to stake out a position for themselves in the market that reflects what the owners and designers truly love.

THE GOLDEN MEAN VS. *ABBASTANZA BRUTTO*

The ancient Greeks debated endlessly about *kalon* or the concept of moral or physical beauty. Aristotle used the term "the golden mean" to judge all facets of a well-lived life and identify the perfect midpoint between excess and deficiency. A plate of food will be neither too hot nor too cold. A house neither too big nor too small. Artwork neither too garish nor too dull. Certainly, this is a good example of how to live a temperate life, and it is one route to an Incanto vision that offers exquisite, perfect beauty. Perhaps a perfectly tailored Armani suit, or the exquisitely well-balanced and refined

Sambonet flatware, stripped clean of all excessive flourishes, produced in Orfengo.

Other philosophers saw beauty as a quality that was less about superficial looks and more about *summetria* or "good," "appropriate," or "fitting proportionality." Others focused on functionality, musing that a wooden spoon was more beautiful than a gold one since it was better suited to its purpose. Socrates, in the *Philebus,* says, "If we cannot capture the good in one form, we will have to take hold of it in a conjunction of three: beauty, proportion, and truth."

From this we might consider that to be truly beautiful, especially in the context of a product one wishes to sell, one's creation must be physically attractive. Even more than that, it also needs to be honest about its nature, ingredients, and provenance, and proportional to the needs of your customer and the moment. Looking through the Incanto lens, I would say that these ancient philosophers are advising us to practice sustainability in our sourcing and manufacturing, and honesty with our customers.

I would add my own insight: true beauty surprises us and creates a feeling of delight when we see it. This is always a tricky balance. Since the 2015 appointment of creative director Alessandro Michele, Gucci has focused on wild, over-gilded, heavily embellished ornamentation and decoration. It's a very personal vision of beauty, a little awkward and sometimes garish. A Gucci garment, at least in this iteration, may appear a little too big for the model, sometimes not terribly functional. Yet, until recently, it was perfectly in alignment with what the brand represents and what its customer wants. As trends have changed, the brand's sales have slipped: Michele has pulled back slightly from his vision, toning down the patterns and stripping away a little of the clashing layers of color. It remains to be seen if his particular dream of beauty will continue to enchant, surprise, and delight his customers.

At illy we have focused on creating a consistent vision of beauty and adding elements on top of it to surprise and delight our customers. We have two forms of packaging: the cans in which we sell our coffee to our customers, and the cups that are used to serve the individual espressos. My elder brother, Francesco, and I realized we needed to differentiate our cups, which serve as our branding and packaging in cafés. After many trials it was finally the architect Matteo Thun who found the perfect shape for the cup by reconsidering it as a piece of art, situated high on the saucer, with the memorable round handle.

Francesco then said, "Why don't we Swatchize the cups?" So, we then commissioned well-known painters like Sandro Chia and James Rosenquist to create paintings on the cups. The first illy art collection of cups was produced in 1992, and every year since new collections are brought to the market. The cost of a collection cup is slightly higher than a traditional cup, but the difference is small if compared with the joy they provide. Too much joy sometimes. Our customers began to leave the cafés with the cups. One lady even put the cup straight into her bag, without drinking the espresso first. Thanks to the cups, we were able to convey to our consumers, "You are drinking something very special." Eventually we grew tired of endlessly replacing the cups when they were stolen and instead offered limited editions of the cups for sale.

This strategy is sometimes categorized as emotional design,[1] whereby a product designer creates a viscerally pleasing object or experience that compels a customer to buy the item and creates a lasting feeling of pleasure and goodwill toward that product. Followers of this theory create a sense of delight by combining visceral, emotional, and reflective design to create an overall experience. Certainly when we approached the design of our cups, we did it in a logical and methodical way. However, there is a specifically Italian approach to beauty in products that is partly about this kind of strategy and is also about a multigenerational passion for a personal and unique vision of beauty that speaks directly and intimately to the customer on an emotional level.

As you consider ways to add a purposeful beauty to your products, think of the humorous styles of Moschino and the quirky Fiat 500. Each exemplifies a unique, ownable aesthetic. Attractive, yes, but always not conventionally *beautiful.* They are arguably the opposite of Aristotle's golden mean with its idealized perfection. Instead, they are closer to what the French might call *jolie laide,* and in Italian would be *abbastanza brutto.* Something that is beautiful in sum, even though the separate elements are flawed and imperfect. This is a second way to look at beauty, one in which Italians have long excelled.

As you consider the aesthetics of your products, ask yourself: Are your products the golden mean? Are they balanced, poised, perfected? Or are they *abbastanza brutto,* a little flawed, perhaps slightly off-kilter, yet still charming and delightful? Either kind of aesthetic standard can be equally appealing or powerful. The most important criteria is to recognize which works best for you and commit fully to it.

BISAZZA

When I thought about the companies that best exemplified Italian ideals of beauty, I had many choices. Companies such as Venini (glass vases), Alessi (kitchen products), Cassina (furniture), and Flos (lighting) all make products of great beauty and originality. In the end, I chose Bisazza for a very personal reason. When I bought my house in the mountains of Alta Badia, I was delighted by the mosaics that decorated all the bathrooms. With a little investigation I found that they had been made by Bisazza, a fairly well-known but still family-run tile company. The tiles of Bisazza are made with glass, cut in perfect squares. The colors are richly pigmented, bright, and lucent. This modern mosaic, like the Roman rabbit or duck emerging from a long-abandoned villa, sparked something in me. I was charmed by the amount of thought, care, and artistry that had gone into the tile. Although the designs are laid down in larger tiles, rather than the ancient mosaics that are laid down square by square, the effect was equally pleasing.

Bisazza, then called Vetricolor, was founded by Renato Bisazza in 1956 in the city of Vicenza. Like all the companies featured in this book, it is still a family business, even as it has grown to have flagship stores all over the world. Mosaic was then a low-tech and low-design field. Most mosaics offered on the market would have been recognizable to the Romans, and not particularly different from the delicate squares of glass used in ancient villas. Indeed, the first product that Vetricolor offered was a tiny 20x20 millimeter square almost identical to those Roman tiles.

Bisazza had either the luck or the foresight to build his first small factory near the city of Murano, famous for its blown glass. Perhaps he was inspired by the vivid swirls of color running through glass vases pulled and modeled into the shape of waves, mottled by air bubbles frozen within the glass. Even though the majority of these small and artisanal glass blowers were primarily creating home decor or small sets of glassware, Bisazza saw an opportunity to do something new. He adapted this material and its production process for an entirely new purpose: as the external cladding of large buildings and skyscrapers. By doing so, he created a new method of decoration for contemporary architecture.

I met with the Bisazza team at the curved entrance facade of their museum, the Fondazione Bisazza. The imposing black exterior wall of the building is covered in the mosaic cladding that made the company famous. It sparkles with color: dusty pink roses and foliage, rendered at a huge scale, dramatic and imposing against the inky background. The museum is full of objects that speak directly to the Bisazza aesthetic: Chandeliers and plates displayed at a scale suited for giants, clad in silver. A retro-modern car, towing an elegant bath, suitable for languorous relaxation. A piece of blue and white Delftware, so large that the figures are human-sized, cut neatly into rectangles that shatter and reform the image as the viewer moves around them. The silhouette of a pure white heart the size of a skate ramp, with a mosaiced MINI Cooper next to it.

For a while, we simply wandered the museum, in awe of the art that surrounded us. Finally, we sat down to talk, and I asked them to consider what beauty and a refined sense of aesthetics mean to them. They pointed out that elegance and beauty are priorities in Italians' lives. It's a habit. When we dress, we don't simply put on clothes to cover ourselves. In many ways we aren't focused on what is good or bad taste so much as the desire to simply pay attention to our appearance. "Getting dressed" every day, in the more formal meaning of the term, is a sign of respect to others. It matters less whether I wear a certain print, color, or style than the simple fact that I paid attention to the details and stepped out of my house looking the very best I can, with whatever I have to work with.

I would argue this idea of "respect" is foundational to an Incanto business. Dressing well, carrying yourself with grace and dignity, are small but crucial facets of a functioning society. People don't have to iron their shirt or shine their shoes before they leave the house. One might do so because one is fastidious about one's appearance. Or it can be a choice one makes to actively improve one's surroundings. Likewise, when we take those extra steps to surprise and delight our customers, it is layered. Part of it is simply our drive to create a better product, but it is also an awareness that everything we do will either improve or degrade the customer's experience and the world around us.

Beauty is key to this because beauty is often seen as optional. This is contrary to Incanto, which insists that products must be beautiful. This beauty takes on a life of its own, changing over the years, but always staying true to the philosophy of "respect," be it to ourselves, our product, or our customer. The Bisazza team elaborated: "Our mother had furniture pieces from renowned designers we didn't like as children, but now we adore! As adults we can now see the elegance, where before we didn't understand. Beauty is a living, breathing thing. It evolves, and it is less about the fashions of the moment than about staying true to your eye, even as your eye matures over the years."

I asked what being a family-run business meant to them, sharing how important my own family's sense of history was to me, and to illy. The Bisazzas concurred. "Our family's genuine passion for the arts is a constant source of inspiration; it stimulates our creativity; it gives us more freedom to experiment. Our collections reflect our aesthetic values: creativity, timeless elegance, contemporary look, lasting quality, and culture."

Like all family-run businesses, this evolves over the generations, and each succeeding generation has a different role in the progression. For Bisazza, this meant that "the founder's vision was to bring back and give new splendor to the art of mosaic, enhancing the quality of the product, introducing a new production technology, while preserving the artisanal side.

"The second generation made the founder's vision evolve, thanks to the collaboration with internationally renowned designers. And finally, our new institute, the Bisazza Foundation, is a huge step, a cultural engagement of the second generation, a legacy for the future, where we can share our permanent art collection with anyone who cares to see it."

In any family business, the choices are strongly linked to the personality, culture, and DNA of the entrepreneur family. This characteristic is specific to family-run companies in Italy, and it is particularly true for Bisazza. Its product is strongly connected with aesthetic and cultural taste.

BEAUTY IN THE EYE OF THE MAKER

Here is a crucial element that Bisazza shares with Luigi Biasetto from chapter 1, "Perfection": a sense of control, and a defined hierarchy that allows the family to maintain control over every detail and ensure the aesthetics of Bisazza remain true to the family's interpretation of beauty.

For Bisazza, like all family-run businesses, it is crucial to have a clear and agreed-upon idea about what makes a product delightful, surprising, or beautiful (remember, coherence!). Certainly, when you tour the Foundation filled with tiled and mosaiced walls that reflect the light and echo one's voice, you feel the intensity of their love for what they do. The family has a shared vision for what is beautiful: rich, vibrant color and bold designs, sometimes at a strikingly large scale.

In their collaborations with artists and architects, they push the mosaic to the limit of what one might think it could achieve, creating mosaic garden sculptures that look like furniture straight out of *Alice in Wonderland* or building a forest of pure white columns to celebrate the work of the architect who designed them.

Throughout my tour of the Foundation, I was reminded of a core element of the Bisazza philosophy: beauty is in the eye of the beholder. The family-run nature of our businesses makes us freer to conceive products that in some way reflect our personality and our taste. This is an important lesson for any product designer or brand manager. Your products need to have a point of view; they need to make an aesthetic choice, be it exquisite, simple perfection, or quirky and idiosyncratic yet delightful. Bisazza continues: "It is likely that great multinational companies, where the personal identity of the entrepreneur is less important and the marketing numbers drive all choices, run the risk of diluting the identity of their product."

Bisazza has a house aesthetic, but they also work with emerging designers and famous artists and architects on collaborations that push the boundaries of what mosaic can be, sometimes beyond even what Bisazza imagines. Every product that Bisazza makes has one thing in common: "aesthetic sustainability." The collection comprises products destined to last over time, not only because of the durability of the materials from which they are made, but because of the aesthetic value of the design itself. This is another facet of beauty: the belief in your vision, and the conviction that it will be relevant long past its production date.

Every great business needs to tell a story about itself. We've talked about the heritage or authenticity of that business.

Striving for perfection is another facet of it. But a firm idea of what is attractive is key to that story. Every great business has an aesthetic. You might not like that aesthetic, but if we are discussing a truly iconic brand, you could probably describe it. Ikea is not to my taste. Indeed, in most ways, it is the opposite of Incanto; but I understand the aesthetic and what the brand, or its designers, consider "beautiful." In this case, efficient, Nordic minimalism. Part of Bisazza's brilliance is in finding designers and artists whose aesthetic melds comfortably with Bisazza's. These collaborations push the boundaries of what the company might normally do. I doubt they ever would have covered a series of MINI Coopers in mosaic without BMW's encouragement (and even then, they were very clear that the display model, now part of their permanent collection, came "without an engine," a wise choice when you are parking a car in a museum literally made of glass).

Incanto beauty can be classic or it can be quirky and unconventional. However, it must in some way reflect the true nature of the product. A beautiful package that disguises a disappointing product will betray the trust of your customer, so make sure that you interpret beauty as another offshoot of augmented quality; something that adds an element of surprise and delight to what you do. True beauty is bold and brave in its conviction, so don't waver in yours.

FOUR

AUTHENTICITY

P erfection. Coherence. Beauty. These are the elements of
Incanto that we have discussed so far. Each reflects a
heritage-focused philosophy of business. Rather than
prioritize short-term returns, Incanto requires a deep and
nuanced understanding of why a business exists, what role
within a community it fulfills, and the direction in which it
should move forward in the coming years. By aiming for perfection, practicing a coherent and holistic view of its operations, and prioritizing a personal and unique vision of beauty,
an Incanto company can stay focused on the long-term
strengths of its business rather than pursuing the ever-shifting
vagaries of the global marketplace.

The belief in the importance of honoring a business's
heritage can be summed up as *authenticity,* a word that has
been diluted and weakened recently. Every MBA graduate
has been taught that consumers crave an authentic experience. Anyone trying to build a personal brand on social
media understands that the approval and the likes depend

on "being authentic." However, this kind of performative authenticity is ultimately shallow and insubstantial. A company that practices Incanto authenticity is not doing so because its marketing department has recommended it, but because authenticity is an integral part of the business's identity. Adopting an inauthentic approach to product development, or manufacturing, or marketing, would be like trying to force two magnets together: nearly impossible without constant pressure to unite two things that naturally repulse each other.

Every idea in this book can be traced back to one core belief: an Incanto business is one that has a deep-rooted story and exists in accordance with the values and principles of that story. An Incanto business has an authentic sense of heritage. As it evolves, all the decisions, products, and choices that the executives and employees make stay aligned with that heritage. Right now, as this global pandemic continues, many businesses are suffering terribly. Yet, the family-owned businesses of Italy, especially those that have stayed close to their roots and have told the same consistent story about who they are and why they do what they do, are surviving and even thriving. There are some simple reasons for this: Focusing on the production of a single category means every resource will go into ensuring the product is still meeting the customers' needs. The family members, especially if the company and the family share the same name, will be committed in a way that employees will not. In difficult times, the entrepreneurs will struggle and make any effort to keep the name of the company elevated.

Finally, the long-term view: In our family-owned company, we plan in terms of generations (each generation meaning twenty years). When difficult times arrive, we think that better times will eventually return. Even though we are losing money now, we will recuperate the losses in the future.

During these periods, it is also normal to use the assets of the family to support the company. It's a kind of symbiosis between family and company that can be incredibly valuable during difficult times.

From a long-term perspective, this makes sense. The roots of many Italian families go back generations. The distant ancestors of today's CEO may have operated the business through the bubonic plague, never mind COVID-19. Family-run businesses have a resilience encoded deep in their DNA that may make them less profitable in the short term, but that allows them to survive for millennia. Indeed, family businesses are estimated to make up 85 percent of modern businesses globally.[1] Today's family businesses tend to have a corporate leadership that understands that they are custodians of something that will outlive them and their children. It means that short-term fixes to "juice" shares or profits are off the table. Instead, all business decisions must continue the company's trajectory in the same dependable and consistent direction. All must be sustainable and work toward the long-term success of the company that will support and care for children and grandchildren far into the future.

For instance, the Agnelli family sold financial assets in other sectors to relaunch (or save) the automotive one when the famed auto executive Sergio Marchionne took the helm at Fiat in the early 2000s. Sustainability has three meanings in this context: First, it is a coherent, long-term view of the company that prioritizes longevity over profits. Second, it is an approach to land and resource management that focuses on old techniques that are inherently regenerative over the use of modern chemical fertilizers and aggressive yield management. And finally, it is socially sustainable, in that it attempts to improve the lives of the people associated with the business.

We'll look at the second definition of sustainability in more depth in a few pages. And, of course, you don't have to look far to find examples of the first. In Brescia, for example, the Beretta family has been managing its eponymous firearms company for fifteen generations. A venture capitalist would throw his hands up in despair at the unrealized profits that could be made by diversifying, selling off portions of the company, diluting standards, chasing down ever cheaper manufacturing in the third world, or investing in unrelated products. But Italian, family-run businesses survive because they stay true to their heritage, tell an authentic story about who they are, and prioritize the long-term survival of a company older than many countries.

YOUNG BUSINESS, OLD SOUL

So, how do you develop a heritage and an authentic story about your business if your business is very young? In the United States, very few family-run businesses go back more than three or four generations. At the time of this writing, even the biggest family-run business in America, Walmart, is less than sixty years old. Walmart, interestingly, does not subscribe to any of the values of Incanto despite being family run for much of its existence (the Waltons currently own less than 50 percent of the company). Instead, the company has adopted what could almost be described as an anti-Incanto approach, for instance, paying employees so little that some must rely on government assistance to get by,[2] and aggressively cutting prices for the brands that it stocks.[3] This strategy has made it vastly profitable, but also vulnerable, since there is no deep sense of loyalty or affection between employee and employer, or customer and store.

One core element of authenticity as seen through the In-canto lens is that a company must prioritize survival over decades and centuries, building a long-lasting and sustainable business in which customers will develop a deep-rooted trust. These businesses are sustainable in three ways: economic, social, and environmental. Part of this is the belief that a business should improve the world it exists in. I don't think anyone would make that claim about a company that replaces countless small-town, local businesses with a monolithic store, paying wages that barely sustain their employees.

At illy, a vastly smaller business than Walmart, my parents and grandfather started the company in 1933, aware of the needs of their employees and willing to help them with their family commitments such as marriage, children, or housing. When I joined illy in 1977, it was normal for the company to give loans to employees to help them buy a new house, pay for their studies, or help their children. As a result, our employees feel a deep sense of loyalty. They want the company to thrive, and their own children to work there one day. This contributes to our sustainability: we hold on to good employees for decades, and we benefit from their years of knowledge. If only Walmart felt inspired to help their employees in the same way.

A young business can have a sense of heritage and be authentic. The key is to understand the ethos of your business. Why does it exist beyond simply profit? Does it prioritize good citizenship by enhancing the lives of the employees, customers, suppliers, and physical neighbors it touches? What does it offer that its competitors don't? What benefit can you give your customers that will earn their loyalty and build a solid base of customers for years to come? Once you have found this core story about your business and what purpose it has in the world, make it central to how you operate

and stick with it, even if the fortunes of your business fluctu-
ate over the years.

One thing that is essential to this kind of philosophy is
understanding that not everyone will accept your version of
"heritage" or agree with what you do—for instance, Ralph
Lauren's Polo line, launched as a line of ties in 1967. The
clothes are good, but the branding seems aspirational rather
than authentic, since a relatively small number of Americans
play or watch the sport. However, Ralph Lauren has committed to this concept and has consistently told the same story
about what Polo signifies. His customers have accepted it.
The Polo line has grown roots. In its own way, it is now authentic enough to convince sufficient numbers of consumers
that its heritage is authentic and its story means something.
Because of this, it will continue to sell—even if I find it im-
plausible and unconvincing.

Americans do not have the same deep connection to the
concept of authenticity that an Italian consumer does. (Although Ralph Lauren opened a stand-alone Polo store in
Rome in 2015, the brand has never become particularly popular here. Why would it, when most Italians have a wealth of
local and trusted tailors and clothiers to choose from?) In
fact, I would argue that the American consumer does not
expect to be treated well, or fairly, by the companies and
brands they purchase, and this provides an opening for a
company willing to try. Italian consumers might not necessarily expect to be treated well (we are a country famous for
sometimes curt service), but they do expect to get a consistent and reliable experience of quality from companies that
their families have patronized for generations.

HOW TO CREATE AUTHENTICITY FOR A YOUNG BRAND

This belief is an important reason the Italians value heritage and authenticity. Why? Because authenticity is reassuring. Think of it as a familiarity that inspires confidence. If my grandparents enjoyed a product many years ago, and the company that produces it still respects the initial values and principles, I will probably enjoy it as well. The perception of quality accumulates over time. This shouldn't discourage you if your company is young. Remember that what counts is the total perception of authentic quality, which is linked partially to the product itself, and partially to the story you tell about the product. And remember that every individual has a preferred way to experience a product. Some of us are visual: quality makes the most impact when it is filled with rich, detailed colors or aesthetically pleasing angles and designs. Some experience quality through touch: cashmere perhaps. Others demand taste above all else, in which case they might prioritize products like Domori. The point is that you have multiple ways to create this story of authentic quality and heritage, and that you have many ways to surprise and delight your consumer. So long as you prioritize the aspect of your business that plays to your strengths and tell a consistent story to slowly build that sense of reassurance and trust.

Your business might not have that long history and lineage, yet you can still apply this idea to how you build and develop your brand. An obvious example in America would be Apple, just under fifty years old, or an airline like JetBlue, which was founded in 1998. Both of these brands have told a consistent and authentic story that reflects their heritage, ideals, and roots. In these cases, authentic means "true": a product made by true people, with true raw materials (natural, not synthetic or counterfeit) through a true process (not by third parties), and a sincere approach to product design, customer service, and quality. In the end, an authentic business can be created either by years or by a consistent, reassuring ethos.

illy had its own experience with creating an authentic sense of heritage and story for a young brand when we bought the vineyard Mastrojanni, which was founded in the middle of the 1970s. A baby by Italian standards! We realized that even though the brand itself was young, its heritage was deep. The land that Mastrojanni was founded on has always been underpopulated and undercultivated. The families that tended to the land used the ancient methods first established by the Etruscans, and later adopted by the Romans. At Mastrojanni the most important operations (pruning, decanting from one barrel to another, bottling) are made when the moon is waning. Why? Because when the moon is waning, the vines reduce their activity. This makes it less traumatic for the plant to be pruned.

Instead of using chemical fertilizers, Mastrojanni uses the green manure approach. Here, the vintners plant herbs that contain the nourishment needed by the soil. When the herbs have grown, the soil is ploughed over so that the herbs will decompose in the earth, nourishing it without the need for any artificial supplements. The farm is certified "integrated agriculture" in accordance with the law of the Tuscany Region. The Ernesto Illy Foundation is promoting a new approach called "virtuous agriculture" aimed at regenerating the soil with organic carbon and reaching a zero-carbon footprint in coffee and other goods farming. Even though Mastrojanni is young, it has a heritage. Today, you can walk along the neat rows of vines and feel in your bones that you are experiencing something similar to what an estate manager would have seen two thousand years ago.

Look at your business through this lens. What traditions are you building on? What brands, individuals, or ideas are part of your company's DNA? In America there has been a wave of "new heritage" brands adopting the iconic history of the nation's industrial past. For example, the bicycle and lifestyle brand Shinola in Detroit, or new boutique whiskey labels like Bulleit Bourbon may be young, but they are building upon a story that feels familiar and reassuring to customers.

Bulleit Bourbon is based on a family recipe, resurrected by a family member a hundred years after the original brewer vanished somewhere between Kentucky and New Orleans. Likewise, Shinola's name comes from a now-defunct shoe polish company that was mentioned in a well-known saying that is too vulgar to print here. Madewell, a highly successful clothing brand in America, is similarly named after an American clothing company that went out of business in the late twentieth century and signifies a level of "Made in the USA" craftsmanship. By aligning new brands with these old names and ideals, these companies can explain who they are succinctly and authentically. Of course, the product must match the description, and this tactic will work only when it is done with sincerity, respect, and a passion for matching or exceeding the quality of the namesake. Customers will give you a chance to tell your story. But they will only give you one chance.

REMEMBER YOUR ROOTS

Understanding your heritage and committing to telling an authentic story about who you are can stop you from making expensive mistakes. In Italy, the pasta maker Barilla forgot the importance of authenticity when it attempted to launch a fruit drink called Alixir, investing more than $12 million in the launch. It failed for two reasons. First, it was incoherent. Why buy one's juice from a pasta maker? But it also felt inauthentic to the consumer. Generations of Italians have trusted Barilla to make a reliably good pasta. It feels familiar and reassuring to open the blue cardboard box. It took them back to their parents feeding them as children. Most adults can gauge the exact quantity of penne or spaghetti to feed their family by looking through the clear film window at the level remaining in the box. There was nothing reassuring about the experience of opening the carton of juice. It felt wrong. My trust in the company did not transfer from one product to another, and the line of juice quickly failed.

AUTHENTIC ILLY

When I started at illy, I made a number of decisions that I thought would strengthen the business. Discontinuing multiple product lines in the name of coherence was one. The second biggest decision I made was equally disruptive, at least at first. My grandfather had the dream of making the best coffee in the world. Back then his customers bought the coffee green and processed the raw beans in small roasting machines at home. Easy to use, these machines usually worked with alcohol or coal, and required only five or ten minutes of hand-cranking. The only danger was under- or over-roasting the beans. The big advantage to consumers was that green coffee beans needed no protection. They could be kept in a paper bag for months without going stale.

If a person bought coffee already roasted, it was from a local roasting company that would put it in a paper bag to bring home. There were no technologies to preserve the roasted coffee, which became stale after a week or ten days. I wouldn't call it undrinkable at that point, but it wouldn't be a good cup of coffee.

My grandfather's greatest innovation was to develop a new way to preserve roasted coffee and ensure that it remained drinkable for weeks or even months. He did this by inventing a method of coffee pressurization, which illy still uses today. We vacuum out the air, then replace it with inert gas, typically carbon dioxide. This special packaging protects the coffee from its two worst enemies: oxygen and humidity. So, as long as inert gas surrounds the coffee, it will stay fresh and taste good.

This guarantee of freshness became an integral part of the story we told our consumers. Yes, our coffee is more expensive, but we can assure you that by the time you take that can home and open it, it will still taste as good as the day it was packaged. Our customers tried our coffee, were reassured by the quality, and became invested in the product. It was now something familiar in their life. Today, they continue to trust us to deliver the same authentic experience: high-quality beans, well packaged, with a superb and consistent taste.

Part of being authentic is accepting that certain product categories will not work for your brand, even as the category grows and seems destined to take over your entire market. Likewise, going after price points that are wrong for your brand, even while they seem important in terms of expansion, is a poor choice. Many years later, I began working at illy after a commercial manager left. He had developed a product line packaged in plastic bags that weren't pressurized. I felt this was not in line with the authentic story of illy; it did not tell a story about exceptional quality. The packaging was fit for a mass-market product, not for a superpremium one. I soon decided to get rid of the whole product line and to refocus on the metallic cans that allowed us to pressurize the coffee.

Likewise, a few years later, we created pods for automatic espresso machines to be placed in offices, factories, and other places of business. The pods were attached to long strips of paper that fed through the machine when a worker ordered coffee. These pods physically worked, but we were mistaken in placing them where we did. The people liked the quality of the espresso but complained about the price. The solution was to place a new manual espresso machine that used the single pod, but only in offices where the higher price was not an issue.

In 1999, illy started a chain of café bars. But we consider ourselves roasters, not managers of cafés. The point of the cafés was to promote the brand, educate the consumer, and present a cohesive story about the whole illy experience. We are not interested in making money selling bottled waters, soft drinks, or beers. Our business is coffee, not food. As a result, it is unlikely we will ever have hundreds or thousands of outlets as some large chains have. Their strategy is to develop the business of cafés and bars, while our strategy is to develop the sales of excellent coffee for the home, restaurants, and other facilities. Although an illy café would seem to make sense, it is not authentic. Here is another way that family businesses are more naturally authentic. Even a large family-run company like illy is limited in the number of projects and ideas it can pursue at once, since our family members are ultimately involved in most decisions. These manpower limitations force us to stay focused on the core truths about who we are and what we do. In our case, we make superb coffee for home and out-of-home consumption.

FERRARI VINEYARD

One reason that Italian, family-run businesses are so attuned to their heritage is simple: we have a lot of it. After all, our country is divided into twenty regions, more than a hundred provinces, and more than eight thousand municipalities. Each one is different from the others, with distinctive traditions and production. We have the highest number of varieties of grapes, apples, pears, cherries, hazelnuts, almonds, and cheeses, just to give some examples. Italy doesn't have a national cuisine but rather eight thousand local cuisines. The recipes are the result of the terroir (where different regions produce crops unique to that area, such as the Vignola cherry, which is unique to Bologna and Modena) and the tradition (the way the ingredients were mixed and cooked). When you understand terroir, it is easy to see why Italian businesses are able to create unique and engaging stories about their heritage. Every story is different and tailored to its immediate audience. I can think of few businesses that have embraced the beauty and joys of their region like Ferrari Trento winery.

In 1902, Giulio Ferrari planted thousands of Chardonnay vines in the high mountains of Trentino with a single-minded determination to create a sparkling wine in Italy that would rival the French champagnes. Fifty years later, after World War II, he searched for someone who could continue his dream since he had no children. From among many pretenders, he decided to pass the Ferrari winery on to Bruno Lunelli, the owner of a local wine store. Thus, in 1952 started the history of the company under the leadership of the Lunelli family. The Trentino Region was recognized as Wine Region of the Year 2020 by *Wine Enthusiast*, in no small part because of Giulio Ferrari's foresight and vision to bring Chardonnay to the area.

The day I visit, I'm greeted by Matteo Lunelli, the third-generation winemaker whose passion for the wines is equal only to his passion for Trentino, the mountain region he calls home. It's easy to see why he loves it so much: Trento, a smaller medieval town that runs between two mountains, opening up to Lake Garda, is almost impossibly beautiful. The old streets are paved in cobblestones and lined with two-story buildings, most balconied, with open windows looking down in a way that is both peaceful and convivial. In the distance, the Dolomites cut a ragged line across the sky, blocking the setting sun and chilling a summer day as the evening draws in.

Matteo tells me that his wine and Trentino are inextricably linked. "Behind every bottle of our wine, you find the culture of Trento and Trentino. It is a *circolo virtuoso*, or virtuous circle. The wine helps the territory, and the territory helps the wine. We produce a mountain sparkling wine, and it is a pure expression of Trentino. We are not making an imitation of champagne, but instead something that is unique."

It is not easy to grow vines in the mountains. Everything must be handpicked, with minimal machinery in the terraced vineyards. They refuse any unsustainable protocols: the Ferrari vineyards are farmed organically, with varietals suited only to sparkling wine production. These demand fresher temperatures to keep a good level of acidity and a high concentration of flavors. The northern, mountainous terroir is perfect for this production. During the day, the vineyards are kissed by the sun, but during the night the cold air comes down from the tops of the mountains that rise a mile into the air. This extreme shift of temperature between day and night creates a distinctive taste and a well-balanced acidity. Life might be easier in the more traditional lowland vineyards, but the final product would not have the finesse of a bottle of Ferrari Trento.

Matteo tells me about how deeply they are linked to their region: "We work with more than five hundred small vine growers and families that supply the grapes to us, and we have established a long-term relationship with them. We ask that they cultivate the land in an organic way: no pesticide or herbicide. At the same time, we are able to pay a premium price for the grapes. It is good to be a supplier for us. We try to protect the safety of the people who work in the land and the winery. The idea is to balance the objective of obtaining high-quality grapes with the need to protect the territory and health of people working in the vineyard. And, of course, the people that benefit the most are the people who work in the vineyard."

I know why Matteo cares as much as he does about the people who depend on him for a living. Still, I ask him to put it in his own words. "It comes from what we believe as a family and something we got from our fathers. It is part of our entrepreneurial culture as a family. We want the company not only to create value for our shareholders but also health, development, beauty for our territory and to make sure that we are a sustainable business. My work as a CEO is a balance of care for my stakeholders and sustainability."

The winery thrives for two reasons. One, the product is exceptional. My preference is for Ferrari Maximum Blanc de Blancs, a sparkling wine made with 100 percent Chardonnay grapes. The single grape, rather than a blend, gives a pure, bold taste (likewise another favorite, the Brunello, which is 100 percent Sangiovese). The wine is what's called a Trentodoc, or a Metodo Classico sparkling wine, which makes the second fermentation in the bottle (as opposed to prosecco, which is fermented in large metal vats rather than individual bottles).

Second, despite its relatively young age, the winery has created a deeply authentic story about what it does, and why it does it. Ferrari's sparkling wine is continually building a presence internationally. As Matteo tells me: "When the customer understands what Ferrari is, there is a lot of brand loyalty. When you are authentic and have authentic values behind your brand, then once your customers understand that, they will be loyal to you." The brand is becoming ever more popular as customers embrace the idea of Incanto that Ferrari represents. Matteo says that sharing the art of Italian living is as important as talking about the wine itself.

The story of Ferrari Trento is the story both of a superb product, created with a passion for augmented quality, and the deep love of Italians for home and land. Matteo and his family feel a profound commitment to improve life for their workers, honor their heritage, and continue to develop the quality of life in Trento. As Ferrari Trento sparkling wine grows more popular, it is also lifting up its region and helping to cement Trento as a destination for wine enthusiasts and connoisseurs. According to Matteo, "We also promote the territory through wine tourism, actively trying to create wealth in the territory that surrounds us."

FIVE
FAMILY

A company, like a family, is built on values. Indeed, families are microcosms of society itself, sharing an emotional perspective of the world, a common culture, and an intertwined economic destiny. A healthy family (or company) is unstoppable. An unhappy, dysfunctional family, on the other hand, is doomed to fracture and fail. Ditto for an ailing and disconnected company.

Nearly all my childhood memories involve illy. The boundaries between the family and our business were faint, and the evening's conversation often revolved around business. After school my siblings and I were often sent to the factory to help in some aspect of production (in retrospect, we may not have been helping as much as we liked to imagine). I talked often with the blue-collar workers, apprenticing with them to understand the nature of their work and absorb their wisdom about their tasks. My first "serious" job was assisting an older worker in refitting the coffee pod machines. From him I learned some basic mechanical skills, and the adage "The fish stinks from the head," something I've always remembered, especially now, as head of Polo del Gusto, the subholding of illy Group that encompasses all the extra-coffee brands (currently Dammann Frères tea, Domori chocolate, Agrimontana preserved fruits, and Mastrojanni wine, and we anticipate expanding further).

When I started working at illy in 1977, the company was still dealing with the consequences of a terrible frost that had killed some billion coffee trees in Brazil, raising the prices by $1.20 to $3.60 per pound. The roasters reacted to this by increasing the quantities of a lower-quality (and lower-priced) coffee called Robusta (a species of coffee tree) to avoid the full impact of the dramatic price increase in the Arabica (the best species). My father was clear. He told us:

> We must fulfill our promise of quality with our customers. We must continue to use only Arabica, despite the impact it will have on the financial statement.

That year we took a loss, the last one I can remember. But our reputation of excellence was saved. We built on this in the following years, recovering the losses and experiencing healthy growth. I have always remembered this moment. My father had a choice. He could have made the entirely reasonable decision to lower the quality in order to keep our products affordable. Instead, he made a difficult decision, suffered financially over the short term, but maintained his promise to our customers.

This deep sense of history, values, and cultural memory is the backbone of the family-run business. At that time, we came closer to failure than at any other point in our history, yet we survived. Every day I carry with me my father's wisdom and the lesson of always fulfilling our promise of quality. I don't know that a larger corporation without that lineage would be able to do so. Would anyone working today in a nonfamily-run business even remember why a long-forgotten CEO made a choice almost fifty years ago? I remember because I admired my father, and his dilemma was one we all discussed together. His belief about quality cut to the core of what our company was and is about. More important, the adults sitting around the kitchen discussing this decision agreed on one thing: no matter what happened, we were all in this together and would succeed or fail as one.

THE ORIGINS OF THE ITALIAN FAMILY

Italians are famed for our close-knit families, and Italy is unique among European societies for the high level of cohabitation, love, and communication between young and old family members. Grandparents are actively involved in their grandchildren's lives, starting as childminders during working hours. These children grow up loved and nurtured by multiple generations within their home, and indeed some still live at home until they marry, sometimes staying well into their midthirties. This trend is becoming more common. By the early 2000s, two-thirds of twentysomething men, for instance, were still living at home, compared to 51 percent ten years earlier. This figure holds true today.

There are multiple and complicated reasons for this. Some economists point to how the Italian public welfare is skewed toward older people, funding pensions but not supporting the young. This same study identified a symbiotic relationship between adult children who wish to be "forever young" and their parents who want to be "forever parents,"[1] continuing to be caregivers and providers even as their adult children move slowly toward independence. In a way this makes sense. Older Italians remember the years of struggle and deprivation after World War II. They grew up in even stricter families, their behavior shaped by religion and social mores that now feel out of date. It is natural to want our children to be unburdened as long as possible by the difficulties of a fully independent life. Add to this youth unemployment, declining marriage rates, and impossibly high rents, and it is logical that children will stay home as long as possible. Finally, Italian parents, unlike their counterparts in Great Britain and America, report that they are simply happier when their adult children live at home.[2]

All of this helps explain why Italian families often go into multigenerational businesses together. What's more, it outlines some of the challenges for a nonfamily business that wishes to replicate some of the advantages of our way of work. For a family business to truly function and last over the generations, there has to be a bigger goal than profits: the primary goal is always the continuation of the family. As previously discussed, we achieve it by prioritizing quality above all else and keeping our promise to the consumers who will, in turn, teach their children to trust our products.

Of course, families can also be dysfunctional. Gucci is a famous example of a business that was almost pulled apart by competing interests within the dynasty. Its core brand was undefined and out of fashion until it hired Tom Ford, and later Alessandro Michele, two designers with wildly different aesthetics who were nonetheless perfectly in tune with their respective times. This speaks to one of the big vulnerabilities of a family-run business: when individual members of a business undermine its health by putting their personal interests before the company. A successful family-run business prioritizes excellence. But when family members begin to see it purely as a financial resource, they put profits first rather than nurture the business. They exploit it. The company's customers will notice the change in quality and abandon the brand. Other businesses falter when faced with a technological advance or social shift they cannot fully understand or resist adapting to. (Kodak in the United States is a classic example of this, although not a family-run business.) The biggest danger, though, is always a poorly managed succession, or one that breeds resentment and anger among the youngest generation.

It is one thing to have a family member who has different ideas. This is nearly always a good thing and is another benefit of a family-run business, since individuals whose ideas are seemingly too radical might not get hired by a more corporate company. However, when an individual family member rejects the values of the family and company, it is problematic. In our case, for instance, illy would not accept a family member who wanted to cut costs and lower quality and prices. That goes against a value that is key to our success. However, a young family member who proposes using technology in a way I do not understand, and perhaps would not initially accept, will always be heard.

NEW BLOOD

The challenge for an existing family-run business is to integrate new blood into the existing group. The challenge for a nonfamily-run business, hoping to emulate the secrets of Incanto, is to create that tight-knit, coherent group identity in the first place. All companies need to innovate in order to guarantee a long life for the brand and the business. Within illy, I am always delighted by the prospect of incorporating new generations; I know they will oblige me to review strategies and change decisions that could be obsolete. But the younger members must first have a good education, and they need work experience (ideally in independent companies unrelated to our own). Finally, when they do join us at illy, they have to demonstrate that what they are suggesting will work.

In our family, we have what might be considered "bylaws" that describe the duties of the following generations. Members of those younger generations have to sign it and act accordingly. If they don't, with the succession, they will only become shareholders. When I was working at the beginning at illy, we only had three customers in the whole city of Rome. I wanted to get more but my father discouraged me. The customers in Rome, he said, were bad at paying their bills. I had to demonstrate that this wasn't true for other potential customers in Rome. Slowly, my father allowed me to add small accounts. When I got them to pay their bills on time, I was allowed to add larger accounts. In a couple of years, Rome was our second largest market in Italy.

Adapting the concept of a family to a conventional, nonfamily-run business is challenging. Ask yourself first what you hope to accomplish and what weaknesses you see in your existing structure. Family is about trust, closeness, a shared vision, and a long-term perspective. It is about adapting your current procedures to allow for long-term growth, sustainable practices, and a multigenerational outlook. If you are not building a business with a view to still being viable in twenty or forty years, why not? If you are not building a business that will retain talented employees for decades, why not?

Then, consider who plays what roles within your corporate hierarchy. Part of a family-run business is understanding that there is a line of succession, and there are procedures in place for ensuring that younger members have a path to move up the ladder. Normally in the family-owned business, every member of the family thinks that he or she is capable of acting as a manager or a director. They think they have an automatic right, that they are entitled. In fact, the sole right you have is to be a shareholder. The rest you must earn. So, you need strong rules in a family business to protect the other employees from the members of the family who think they have more than their allocated share of power. Never put relatives in hierarchical positions over one another. It can cause strife; it can also lead to one relative feeling compelled to cover the mistakes of a loved one. That rule should be applied to all the family members, not only to the owners.

In this respect, a family-run business is different from a corporation: because we are obliged to deal with one another outside of the working environment, we are obliged to constantly watch out for abuse, mismanagement, or any kind of suboptimal behavior. I have seen many nonfamily-run businesses in which inept or unaccomplished managers are allowed to fail time after time until finally they fail so spectacularly that they are fired or removed. In a family-run business, after a father will come the son, the cousin, the grandchildren, and so on. As each generation makes way for the next, the values that were established years ago are passed on. On a deep, visceral level we understand we are nothing without those core values. Family-run businesses have too much at stake to allow bad managers to derail operations or incompetent people to fail for decades.

As you look at your own business, ask yourself about that core value. What is the essence of your business and brand that you would pass down to your successors? Value it, treasure it, and never compromise.

ZEGNA

Although I prefer to dress informally, there are many occasions when I must dress more formally. Perhaps a meeting or an appearance that requires an attitude of sophistication or elegance. On these occasions, I am nearly always in a suit made by Zegna, a family-owned, luxury men's clothing company that epitomizes the quintessence of Italian style. Their suits are soft, yet as solid as their leisurewear. Somehow the fabric manages to be both warm in the winter and fresh in the summer. I can wear a Zegna garment all day, and it will never crease: the hallmark of truly fine fibers.

Founded by Ermenegildo Zegna in 1910, Zegna is an example of the two ways that Italian businesses operate as a family. First, literally. To date, four generations of Zegnas have owned and operated the business. The current generation is doing a superb job. Second, as an extended family. Ermenegildo Zegna came from the Biella province in northern Italy. The business is still closely associated with the area and feels a great sense of responsibility for the people, the territory, and the environment of Biella.

I meet a third-generation family member, Anna Zegna, now president of Fondazione Zegna, at her country house. It's a pleasant summer day. There is a busyness in the air and, in the distance, the sound of construction. She tells me crews are currently repaving the roads around the factories, even though Zegna does not own them. They are actively restoring the environment in Trivero, where Zegna is located, planting trees and fortifying the land. This is done simply because the family feels a sense of responsibility for both the land and the people who live there. They are continuing their grandfather's belief that everything they do must ultimately leave the land, and the people of the area, better than they found it.

Anna, like me and my family and all the other families featured in this book, is deeply connected to her sense of family history. She knows the origin story of the Zegna business well. The early days set the tone for how her family operates now. She tells me how she has studied her grandfather's life and come to learn that, for him, the concept of quality was embedded within his soul. Ermenegildo Zegna came from a simple background. He was the tenth son of a very simple couple. They lived on a farm with chickens. He was the youngest child, but somehow he had something unique: a purpose in life, a passion for quality that stemmed directly from how he saw the world. That quality is hard to define. For certain people, quality is in the details of everyday life and the way they approach living. Others do not care so much about quality, and they live well anyway.

"For my grandfather Ermenegildo, it was really a mission," Anna Zegna tells me.

And his idea was not to copy, not to reproduce the others, but to create something unique. And we've held onto that vision. In our family, every generation has built something on top of the previous one. So, my grandfather produced the wool fabric, my father and uncle's generation did the ready-to-wear and started to go outside of Italy to sell the products. Now, my brother Gildo—our CEO—and other members of our generation are making the next step, directly operating stores all over the world. My nephew Edoardo, Gildo's son, had his own digital marketing business in the US. So, it was natural to bring him on board to launch the new omni-channel project for Zegna, which means that the touchpoints today are not only the store but zillions.

Today, Edoardo is the innovation and consumer strategy director.

At Zegna, as at illy, each generation progresses on the work of the previous generation. And because we see ourselves as part of a long line of people working toward the same goal over multiple generations, there is no temptation for new CEOs to "make their mark" by radically reshaping a strategy that has worked well for hundreds of years. Likewise, we do not experience the disruption that many companies endure when a new CMO comes on board.

Often, these high-level creative executives will only be with a company for a few years. They may have one eye on the door, looking to make short-term, radical changes simply to prove to the board or the shareholders of their next company that they are "visionaries." Family-run businesses are less susceptible to this kind of thinking, partly because of our deep, granular knowledge of what has worked (or failed) for our business decades or even centuries ago. This makes us more adaptable because we have the historical perspective to feel confident in the wisdom of our decisions in making a bold move.

This belief also compels us to care for the world around us in a way that is less likely for a conglomerate, or privately held company. Anna tells us how:

Sustainability has been important since the beginning, when my grandfather began planting the first of what would be five hundred thousand trees to compensate for clearing a large area for a wool mill. Then he paid attention to the workers and the local community. My grandfather built a swimming pool for the local community, and gymnasiums and cafeterias. Today his vision is responsible for Oasi Zegna, a nature preserve thirty times the size of Central Park that is dedicated to Ermenegildo's idea of "green thought." Recently, to celebrate our 110th anniversary, we decided to plant more trees in Oasi Zegna. We do this to continue my grandfather's work of preserving and enhancing the environmental resources. I imagine my grandfather, in 1939, looking at this empty landscape and having the vision to imagine it as it is now, would be pleased.

A family business won't last long if it doesn't extend the concept of family to the people who work the land, manufacture the product, and whose lives intertwine with the family who owns and operates the actual business. I can think of no company that understands this more than Zegna, which actively works to better the lives of these extended family members.

GIVE AND GET BACK

The core of this belief system is the idea that *we get something and then we give back*. This is multifaceted. It can mean caring for your employees or caring for the land and natural resources that your company depends upon and seeding the ground for a better future. The Ermenegildo Zegna Founder's Scholarship is in its eighth year of providing financial assistance to Italian students wishing to spend time abroad, acquiring valuable know-how and experience that can be brought back to Italy, thereby contributing to the country's future development.

In 2010, the psychologist James Hillman wrote an essay called the "Ethics of Quality" for the Zegna centennial. Anna points out one line that she loves especially: "the nature of luxury derives from the luxury of nature." She thinks about it for a minute, then tells me, "Luxury, which for me is also quality, is really inspired from nature."

To prove the point, Anna shows me a picture of the trees in Oasi Zegna changing colors, from green into fantastic gold, yellow, orange. It is as if nature surrounds you and overwhelms you with its beauty. Her love of the land and her deep commitment come through as she talks about the beauty of this rare and special place. And really, all places that are in some way involved with an Incanto business must be looked at as rare and special. This is particularly true when you are considering how you source the exceptional materials that go into your products.

Like illy, Zegna relies on superlative raw materials. It has a system for recognizing and rewarding the very best suppliers who produce the finest, strongest yarn. And, like illy, Zegna is thinking ahead, pondering how climate change may or may not affect its business in the future. Much of its wool is sourced from Australia, which is currently in the grip of a long drought. As Anna explains: "It's very hot. So, how do you keep your pastures, how do you keep your animals, how do you take care of your flock? And this can't be done by spoiling the landscape you are living in. So, a lot of education is required."

This is where a superb supply channel intersects with a family-like relationship. Just as we are working ever harder to ensure our suppliers are resilient as they face a challenging and unpredictable future, so, too, must Zegna collaborate with its suppliers as the world grows hotter and drier. Anna emphasizes how important it is to communicate with these far-off ranchers. "The more quality you are asking for from your suppliers, the more you need to give them feedback on what works. Otherwise they will not be able to give you the continuous improvement in quality you need."

Constant, friendly, direct communication is key. After all, what is a functional family but a group of individuals who feel free to talk openly with one another? This is family writ large, the recognition that on a macro level we are truly all in this together. This philosophy applies to everyone who works directly at Zegna.

Anna's brother, Gildo, often says that Zegna is a family business and a private company that is managed like a public company in the sense that it's flat, transparent, shared, and very rewarding. Zegna uses a 360° communication philosophy to share news, goals, and objectives with the employees, be they white-collar workers, factory workers, or salespeople. According to Anna, "This 360° system means that Zegna is a family business, yes, but all of our thousands of employees are part of our larger family."

Like illy, and our control over which of our cafés and restaurants get signage and other illy-branded items, Zegna realizes the importance of making sure its voice is clear to the customer. And like us, it found that when its product was sold primarily through independent stores, that voice was getting diluted. "Some stores that carried Zegna were mainly focused on business suits, others mainly on sportswear," Anna says. "And because we think we are all designers in Italy, the owners of these stores would give a personal interpretation to the brand, which was not respecting what the vision of the collection was."

In 2010, Zegna opened a shop in Milan, designed by Peter Marino, the famous architect who also designed Chanel, Louis Vuitton, and Bulgari. Marino is known for a particular point of view in the design, taking the identity of the brand and bringing its signs and visuals to the architecture. Now, when you walk into a Zegna store, you feel you're in a men's lifestyle store. There is a lot of wood and natural shapes interspersed with a curated selection of clothing. The blend of the environment and the product creates a special energy that makes each collection reveal a certain kind of atmosphere.

Running a family-owned business is largely about values. For Zegna, and for illy, too, those values are in the DNA of the brand. Anna reflects often on her grandfather's roots in the country. A love of and respect for the wild, natural world is key to literally everything the brand does. Zegna's social media feed features as many pictures of Oasi Zegna as it does of the clothes.

So, the lesson here is that any brand, company, or business needs to know what the core truth of its DNA is. This truth will function as your guide, helping you to prioritize difficult choices and keeping you faithful to a mission of augmented quality, even when those around you wish to dilute it. So, what does your company—and by extension, your family—believe in? What principles guide you and shape what you do? These values do not need to be exclusive to family-owned businesses, of course. You can apply them to whatever you do. Anna breaks it down elegantly: "First of all, there's vision. Vision gives you something that goes beyond where you are and is something that comes from within. There's something within you that drives you from inside to create this idea. When you begin, your vision is blurred. You almost can't define it when you start a new project. But it has to be authentic, which means that it relates to who you are as a person, as a brand, as a company. So, it needs to be consistent to what you really are within your personality. And finally, everything starts from your passion, because without passion there's no way you can meet the challenge and the failures."

Another crucial element is a deep knowledge about the heritage of your category: what came before you, how it succeeded, how it failed, and how you can improve on it.

"Unless you know exactly all the process and you know how to design (in our case) the perfect men's wardrobe," says

Anna, "you can't break the rules and create something completely different."

Finally, that knowledge extends to your customers. Anna continues: "The biggest heritage and the most important value of the company are our customers. Yes, you can continue to build up new customers, but first of all you have to really, continuously, connect and interface with your existing customers because these are those that love the brand, that will come back, and that will grow with you. There's the golden rule in Zegna that customers are central."

As we wind up our conversation, Anna shares a final key part of her philosophy, *technē*, the Greek word for a mixture of beauty, intuition, and technology. Like me, she believes that technology can be a great aid to a well-lived life and a well-run company. Zegna's #UseTheExisting campaign promoted the brand's commitment to sustainable products using both natural and "technical" fabrics and innovative processes—all in service of a goal of zero-waste production.

However, technology must also be tempered with beauty and intuition. I think this balancing act is the final attribute of a family-run business. Because we are directly in touch with that historical, cultural DNA of who we are, we are more comfortable trusting our intuition. After all, that intuition is based on our knowledge of every success, failure, or lesson learned over the course of our family's business. As you move forward, look for ways to uncover, understand, and adopt the DNA of your business. Enshrine it within the culture of your company and use it as your guide to make good choices in difficult times.

S I X

SIMPLICITY

M any years ago, my wife and I considered buying a certain kind of microwave oven to upgrade our kitchen. The oven itself was wonderful: it cooked evenly, heated the food precisely to the degree specified, and had clean elegant lines that would fit perfectly into the minimalist 1950s aesthetic of our weekend home. My wife and I were almost certain: this was it. Until she asked, "How do we turn the beeps off?" With every press of a button, the oven beeped. If you needed to raise the temperature, the oven beeped with every five-degree increment. If you wished to set the timer, or adjust the clock, the oven beeped with every minute you added. After a few minutes, we could no longer bear to hear the beep.

Soon we realized that the microwave oven had multiple layers of unnecessary functionality. The instruction booklet was as long as a bedside novel. The automated settings were apparently limitless. We asked the salesperson if he could disable the beeps and explain the instruction manual to us. Eventually we admitted defeat and chose a simpler model, to the astonishment of our salesperson. He pointed out again that the first oven was the most modern option in the store. The instructions were complicated to give users more options. The beeps were to assist us, and he had no idea how to disable them anyway.

Years later, I met a CIO (chief innovation officer) from a big American tech firm. During a conversation about product design, I mentioned how aggravating I had found this oven and its convoluted instructions and incessant beeps. "Why are they designed like this?" His answer was simple: Most product engineers are extremely rational and logical people; sometimes excessively logical. For them, the endless programming options offered choice and flexibility, which all customers want, right? Furthermore, the beeps offer a logical and desirable benefit in letting the user know that the oven is working as designed. Each beep reassures the user that the desired input has been acted upon. Because they don't see any potential downside to the options and choices and technology, it is impossible to imagine that anyone else will see a downside. So, they keep designing kitchen products with the infernal beeps, despite the aggravation they cause to frequent users.

At the illy office, we had a similar problem when a well-meaning office manager decided to purchase a three-in-one printer, fax machine, and scanner. She explained that this new machine would take up a fraction of the room of three bulky pieces of equipment. All our junior and administrative staff were educated on the machine. Within a day, their scans and faxes and printouts were hopelessly jumbled, the various staff members were up in arms about their coworkers hogging the machine, and the previously well-functioning office was melting down over something that should have been simple and fundamental.

I think both the American product designers and our own office managers lost sight of something obvious. An improvement is sometimes less about adding more functions than it is about stripping away functions that add unwanted complexity. Simplicity is often perceived unconsciously. We may "see" elegance and refinement, but what we are really admiring is simplicity and the promise that simplicity makes to us of subtracting a layer of distraction or frustration from our lives. When choosing a durable good like a kitchen machine, a suit, a bag, or a car, simplicity is something that consumers are looking for even if they don't realize it. Most of us like things that are simple to use and that can be used intuitively, without reading the instructions. The iPhone, or any Apple product, is an obvious example of this. How liberating it is to buy a tech product that is so intuitive to use it needs no instructions. Ditto with Ikea and its stick-figure directions. Complexity is often a distraction; it hides the failures or weaknesses in what you are doing. If your product requires hundreds of pages of directions to instruct the customer how to use it, then your product is flawed. Likewise, if your flavors need added elements to make them palatable, something is fundamentally wrong with what you are doing. Remember our Boeing example? The fact that the aircraft was literally not airworthy without an added software upgrade should have suggested there was something deeply wrong with it. A plane should not require an added level of complexity to make it work safely, especially when the complexity confuses the pilots in critical and dangerous moments.

ITALIAN SIMPLICITY

I believe Italians love simplicity. True, we invented the extravagant and intricate baroque style in the 1600s and spread its gold leaf overlays and artwork all over Europe. But at our core, we are people who understand the value of very good raw materials that require little or no processing or improvement to be enjoyed. There are few dishes I have eaten in my life that I still remember years or decades later. One is the risotto alla Milanese by Chef Gualtiero Marchesi. Another was a simple dish: cooked vegetables with extra-virgin olive oil, served in a restaurant close to Cuneo. It was so tasty, so balanced in flavors between the vegetable and the oil that I will remember it for the rest of my life. The vegetables were pared back to their very essence; the textures (crunchy here, soft and silky there) surprised with every bite. The subtle sweetness of the squash, and the unexpected tartness of the tomatoes meant that every taste was slightly different, even without any added flavorings. This is a classic example of the short-recipe philosophy that we apply to everything we produce at illy. It is the essence of why simplicity is often more compelling than complexity.

Chef Marchesi's kitchen was likewise pared back to the essentials. His risotto alla Milanese was made with rice, saffron, and few other ingredients. The process to cook it was quite simple as well. Simplicity means you can hold on to the basic tools that allow you to do your job and shed anything superfluous (or ideally avoid purchasing them in the first place). An Italian kitchen most likely doesn't have any particularly complex gadgets, such as an electric pressure cooker, a sous vide immersion cooker, or an air fryer. But we do have knives, pans, and pots for specific tasks. A *passaverdura* (food mill) to separate the bones from the flesh in a fish soup, or the seeds and skin from tomatoes. A tall, narrow vessel that allows water to quickly return to the boil once you add your pasta, Dutch ovens for anything that needs unhurried cooking and even heat distribution, like stews or beans. A *mezzaluna*, or half-moon knife, that minces garlic and herbs with a rocking motion. A *padella,* or sauté pan, with its deep, curved sides, for sautéing meat.

Many of these knives and pots and pans will have been passed down over the years, perhaps dented or chipped from decades of use, but full of memories and treasured because our parents and grandparents once used them to feed us. As we cook, stirring pots on the stovetop, we are constantly tasting and refining what we make. We season and flavor with a light touch as needed. Simplicity in the kitchen requires the best ingredients, tools suited for the work, and vigilance from the cook.

Of course, simplicity in business requires the same.

SIMPLICITY IN THE BUSINESS LIFE

As you seek out new products and new markets to expand your business, vigilance is essential. Most large European businesses will eventually consider expanding into the United States. Some with success, some otherwise. In 1980, my father decided to try selling espresso in Phoenix, Arizona. We reasoned that there were already many Europeans living in New York City and San Francisco who appreciated espresso and would be interested in trying our product. But before expanding to these cities we wanted to understand if an American unaffected by European attitudes and opinions would also appreciate our espresso. We were confident that our product's quality was superior to the other coffees available to these consumers.

We decided to create a new product for American consumers: an espresso machine specifically for restaurants and hotels. We were already using a similar product to great success in the Netherlands, Germany, and France. With a few tweaks in the electronics, we figured that the US market would love it just as much. The machine was heavy duty and not exactly a thing of beauty. It was also manual, which we did not realize would be a problem. But very quickly, our new clients reported back to us that their bartenders and waiters, unlike their counterparts in Europe, did not have the time to stand vigilant over the coffee cup, turning the machine off at the perfect point (roughly twenty seconds), just as the cup filled to the correct depth. Instead, they would run to serve another table or pour another drink. The cup would run over, and the coffee would be ruined. We took the machines back and reconfigured them with an automatic feature, but now they began mysteriously shorting out at random points of the day because they weren't built to handle American power surges. Eventually we fixed this problem, too, but at great expense and frustration.

I took two lessons from this. The first was that I had made my life, and the challenge of expanding into the United States, overly complex. From that moment forward, I never again attempted to introduce a new product into a new market. Instead, we focused on one or the other. Second, I realized that simplicity could mean different things to different markets. Our European customers appreciated the control that the manual machines gave them. Their staff members were themselves connoisseurs of good coffee. They took pride in perfectly timing the brewing cycle, standing guard for the exact moment to flip the switch and finish the brew. Our American customers did not have the time or the same feeling toward coffee that we did. For them, our simplicity was a flaw. It made life more complex.

Even though we eventually created a product that worked for our brand, I realized the importance of simplicity. If you start simply, you can educate your customers and win them over until they are familiar enough with your products that they no longer require explanation.

STAYING SIMPLE IN THE FACE OF COMPLEXITY

Some companies get sidetracked by thinking that the more ingredients (or elements) you add, the more consumers you will satisfy. The real pasta al pomodoro is made only with spaghetti, tomato sauce (cooked with some garlic), and olive oil, with parmigiano cheese and fresh basil on top. Adding other spices will maybe satisfy the people who love them, but will disappoint the connoisseurs who know how it should be made.

Of course, if you are going to offer a product this simple, it must be of exceptional quality. However, you must also accept that you cannot satisfy all of your potential customers. You must segment consumers, focus on the chosen segment, and produce the right products for these people. Few companies have this strength and integrity; they normally try to please everybody. The global competition is bringing to the market products that perfectly fit each segment. If one tries to satisfy everybody, probably in the end one will satisfy nobody.

The Agnelli family is a good example of how simplicity can refocus a sprawling and struggling business. One of the most famous families in Italy, this family epitomizes glamour, romance, and a decadence that is hidden from sight by private jets, private trains, palatial walled estates, and membership in the highest society of both Rome and New York. Truman Capote adopted Marella Agnelli as one of his "swans." She and her husband, Gianni, summered with Capote and John and Jackie Kennedy in Amalfi. Indeed, my generation describes the Agnellis as "the Italian Kennedys" (perhaps outdated now, though I wouldn't compare them to America's current most famous family, the Kardashians). Either way, they loom large in our consciousness and our cultural history, and their businesses touch most of our lives on a daily basis.

Agnelli is the parent company of Fiat, founded in 1899. The business eventually grew to be one of the most important companies in Italy. In 1923, it took over Juventus F.C., the most famous Italian football team. By the second half of the twentieth century, Fiat employed more than 100,000 people and had made almost 1.5 million cars. The company expanded, investing in other iconic Italian car brands, including Ferrari, and buying Chrysler in America. It diversified in many other sectors including publishing (purchasing the Economist Group) and real estate. Company leaders were so busy with this rapid and sprawling expansion that, like Benetton, they failed to see just how much a threat Japanese and German competitors were to their central business, cars. Even as one existential nightmare loomed, another hit them straight on when the company experienced the great fear of any family-run business: losing their presumptive heirs to unforeseen events. In 1997, Giovannino Agnelli, the nephew of Gianni, died of cancer. And in 2000, Gianni Agnelli's only son, Edoardo, killed himself at the age of forty-six.

In the early 2000s, the Agnellis were in even greater danger of losing control of Fiat due to a large loan that could not be repaid. Luckily they were able to tap into their investment portfolio, pay off the debts, and keep control of the company. However, the thought of the Agnelli family losing control of its core brand and the company that started it all was shocking.

The company decided to refocus on cars and, thanks to the great manager Sergio Marchionne, saved Chrysler by merging it with Fiat, now known as FCA. It is again a successful company, and is currently in the process of merging with the French Peugeot. After the merger, the name became Stellantis.

The lesson here is that even a business as large as the Agnelli empire can lose focus and set aside simplicity in pursuit of ever larger goals. Either way, at the turn of the century, when the company was at its most vulnerable, a lack of focus threatened its long-term viability. By pulling focus back from distractions and other "pet projects" and concentrating on Fiat, the family was able to solidify the Agnelli empire for good.

THE FOCUS DIVIDEND

One way to consider this in your own business is to look at it through the lens of a "focus dividend." According to this concept, when we are short a resource, be it time to complete a project, money to finance it, or any other necessity one would normally require to be productive, we are unexpectedly more productive than if we had everything we needed easily and freely available. If you look back on your life, there may well have been a moment where you clearly did not have the money, time, materials, or other elements to successfully complete a project. And yet you did. Companies often simplify when, as with Agnelli, they are in trouble. If you find yourself struggling in this unfocused, uncertain predicament, make sure you understand that you have an opportunity here. If you set aside your fears and anxieties about what lies ahead and simply use all the resources at hand, you may find that you work in a more focused, more logical, and more successful way.

In my own experience, I have found that facing an impossible situation—for example, when we did not have the funds or the time to successfully complete a necessary project—often leads to unexpected success. It turns out that you don't need as much as you thought you did, and the urgency of the moment cuts through the chatter and distractions that normally fill your day. When you look up from your work, you realize you have accomplished it.

Part of simplicity is preemptively applying this concept of focus dividend to your business. What elements of your budget or your product lines or your way of doing things are you telling yourself are "essential"? Perhaps they aren't. Now, I'm not suggesting that you use this as an excuse to demand more work out of your employees or to cut down on their benefits or privileges. Rather, consider if there are outdated or unnecessary aspects to your process. Do you really need that weekly meeting between all branches? Can you apply some of the lessons of 2020? Many employees are just as productive without constant physical oversight from their department heads. Can you streamline old, unnecessary ways of doing things? What layers of distraction are impeding your business from moving forward and evolving in the post-pandemic world?

Even more interesting, what are you wrongly assuming your customer wants from you? And are you offering things that are unnecessary, overly complex, or counterintuitive to your customers' desires? Just as I eventually bought a microwave oven that did one thing well rather than the more complex model that baffled me, so might your customers prefer you to streamline your offerings. Is there a way to save money by letting go of the unnecessary and reinvesting in those things your customer truly prioritizes? I still think of a simple vegetable dish with flavors shining so bright that I've never been able to replicate them. Do you have an opportunity to offer something similar to your customers?

SEVEN
CULTIVATION

One of my joys in life is visiting our various estates and businesses. Unless something has gone terribly wrong or there is a problem to fix, it is delightful to visit these rural places, where our raw materials, perhaps olives or grapes, are slowly nurtured on trees or vines. Because we practice "green" agriculture, we encourage most of the local birds and small animals to remain on the land (unless they harm the crops). Native herbs and grasses are allowed between the rows of vines; eventually they will be turned over to fertilize the soil naturally. When I drive to Montalcino to visit our winery, Mastrojanni, I like walking early in the morning in the vineyards. Often, I meet some roe deer, a hare, or a pheasant, and I'm pleased to see that everything is perfectly in order, both with our business and the natural world.

One of my responsibilities is to constantly cultivate and nurture all the brands in the Polo del Gusto universe (see chapter 5, "Family," for more information). Like a farmer, I must make sure that every element of our company is healthy, that the different cogs of our business are aligned with one another, that a hard frost or a dry summer doesn't cause chaos throughout our supply chain. This "cultivation" is more layered though. I must also cultivate the culture of the company. Within our offices and factories, I must culti-vate a sense of shared purpose and contentment among our employees. To this end, I try to know as many of our employ-ees as I can: hear them when they are unhappy, understand why they may be frustrated. Finally, it is up to me to cultivate the overall vision of what we do and why. There have been a dozen times over the past fifteen years when I could have radically changed what we do, and when we could have made a move to become a vastly larger business. In this alternate version of illy, we might have built thousands of cafés instead of hundreds; or sold less-expensive versions of our products to expand our reach.

There are two simple reasons illy will never expand in such a drastic way: As long as we insist on the very best raw materi-als, we will be limited in the quantity we can produce. As long as we use more demanding, lower-temperature processes to refine our cacao and coffee, we will be a smaller company than the big international brands, whose products are avail-able on every city block from San Francisco to Sydney to Sin-gapore. This is a purposeful choice, and one that is core to who we are as a company. Sticking to this choice requires cultivation. It means I need to stay engaged with our employ-ees, family members, and suppliers to ensure we are all in agreement on this vision. To that end, I travel to our various plantations when I can.

It is easy to visit a winery in Tuscany, but more complex to travel all over the world and visit our other plantations. Most—our cacao, coffee, and tea partners—are in remote, mountain-ous places. Most are family-run businesses themselves—people we have worked with for decades. Some are perched on the green, tropical hills of Venezuela and Ecuador. The tea plantations of our supplier are in India, China, and Sri Lanka. It has taken decades to build relationships with plantations and families who have similar beliefs to ours.

INCANTO IN ECUADOR

There is nothing quite like stepping out of an air-conditioned car and onto a cacao plantation. The tropical heat is overwhelming. The lush native vegetation, mixed with the higher elevation, and the small plantation houses have a timelessness about them. I feel the contrast to my life in Italy, but also a sense of continuation. These people, working hard to nurture the trees and harvest their crop, are in alignment with my own business. Domori has partnered with two plantations, one in Venezuela called Hacienda San José, where we are 50/50 partners with the Franceschi family. The Franceschis are originally from the French island of Corsica but have lived in Venezuela for almost two hundred years, farming and trading cacao. The other plantation, Hacienda San Cristobal, is in Ecuador.

There is one truth about chocolate that any grower must understand and accept: cacao is about genetics. If your tree is good, and you give it the correct care, you will get good cacao. If your tree is bad, nothing you can do will make it grow decent cacao. This is the opposite of grapes, where one genetic strain can produce stellar wine at one vineyard, but a few miles away, in a different microclimate or subtly different soil, make wine that is dull, lifeless, and a chore to drink.

The very best species of cacao is Criollo, representing less than 0.1 percent of global production. It requires a longer time and more care to process. For most chocolatiers it is not worth the extra effort, especially when the finished product is more expensive than the commercial chocolate consumers are used to. For us, though, Criollo is as close to our hearts as the Arabica bean. More difficult, more expensive, sometimes frankly hard to work with, but undeniably better.

Venezuela is currently too dangerous for me to visit as I am at risk of being kidnapped, or robbed. However, I have been lucky to travel to Hacienda San Cristobal in the southern Guayaquil area of Ecuador, not far from the sea. A wonderful hilly area that used to be rain forest and is now devoted to agriculture, you will find many coffee and cacao plantations there. To get the best quality and a satisfactory productivity, the plantation, like the vineyards, is high density. A few towering kapok trees, the last survivors of the old rain forest, watch over us and the landscape, now smoothed out into ordered rows of cacao trees. The plantation is clean and calm, with more birdsong than machine noise. At noon, in the steamy heat of the day, the whole plantation retreats under the shade of the trees, napping and eating, and holds its breath until it is cool enough to commence work again.

It is a joy to watch these expert harvesters move down the lines of trees. They swiftly machete down the *cabosse* (the cacao fruit) from the tree. Next, holding the *cabosse* in one hand and the machete in the other, the worker cuts the fruit in the middle lengthwise. Then, with the point of the machete, she pushes the beans out of the two halves of the *cabosse*. The whole operation takes a few seconds, with a speed that reminds me of a juggler.

Finally, the beans are put to one side, in a series of wooden boxes where they slowly begin to ferment, forming a foaming white substance and a strange and unexpectedly sweet and pungent smell. The geckos and other lizards are drawn by the scent, and workers futilely try to swat them away. The beans are eventually spread out to dry under the shade of the trees. Few people realize how crucial this step is. If the beans are overheated while they dry or are contaminated by the soil, they will be essentially worthless. So, the final drying operation is done on cement flooring and under a shady canopy to avoid burning. In Ecuador, thin clouds high in the atmosphere diffuse the sun's rays, protecting our precious crop from a burn that would ruin its quality.

Finally, the beans are weighed and bagged, ready for delivery. Throughout the process, the workers remain calm; they know that it's more important to do things right than quickly. Well trained and motivated, they work diligently through the last light of the afternoon to finish the task.

THE END RESULT

A few weeks later, the beans arrive in Italy and are processed through the factory as either blends or "single bean" bars. The latter are my favorite because they allow you to experience the subtle differences between the Criollo strains. Try a piece of Domori chocolate: you might initially be surprised to see that it is lighter than most high-cacao brands. Instead of dark brown or black, our chocolate is the light brown color of a monk's robes. Why? Because, like our coffee, we roast at lower temperatures and the beans stay light in color. Often, a new customer asks whether the chocolate is truly good quality, because they associate lighter bars with milk chocolate. I explain that milk is primarily used to mask poor-quality cacao, and we seldom use it. Neither do we add cacao butter to our chocolate, which is like adding water to wine. We would never dilute the taste and flavor simply to produce more chocolate.

Still, they look at it in confusion. Years of middle-market "quality" chocolate has taught them to associate dark chocolate with a high standard.

The way I see it, helping your consumers develop their own understanding and appreciation for what you have grown or created is the logical final step of the cultivation process. So, when they ask if it is good, I encourage them to taste.

First, they unwrap the small, square bars and break off a corner. Often, people are surprised at the simplicity of it. There are no sea salt crystals, or bacon. No crystallized ginger, turmeric flakes, dried fruit, spices, or dehydrated raspberries. There are no swirls of color, or pieces of hot pepper. Some, who enjoy these novelties, are disappointed initially. But I explain: if you give the chocolate your attention, you will taste all these elements and more, simply because a great cacao bean is as layered and multifaceted in flavor as a noble grape or a well-aged cheese.

Try our Chuao bean chocolate, a variety of Criollo. First, it melts into a soft, lemony note: bright citrus, without any astringency. As the lemon fades, the chocolate blooms into a cloud of blackberry, which finally finishes on a strong, almost herbaceous note. Our Porcelana, another variation of Criollo, is our most delicate bean: hard to grow, but so richly sweet and fragrant; it naturally smells as if some cream were added. A bite of this chocolate—rarely produced and only ever in very small quantities—is full of hazelnut, vanilla, and even notes of bread crust. Finally, they might try a small piece of the ancient Guasare, a strain of Criollo that was originally found along one riverbank in Venezuela's Sierra de Perijá mountains. The Guasare is considered the "father" of all the other Criollo varieties that derives from it. The chocolate fills the senses with notes of rose, caramel, and cream.

Each of these bars is a miracle: these beans were dying out, forgotten and ignored because they were too demanding and difficult to grow. Every strain that we preserve and fortify, planting more trees and contracting with more farmers, feels like a victory both for us and for these precious and extraordinary plants. Every time we plant these rare beans, we are ensuring the genetic diversity that will allow cacao to become more resilient to climate change, pollution, and insects.

Careful, considered cultivation can do this for your business too. Look at your supply chain and identify areas where you can actively cultivate better raw materials. Are there ways to diversify the "strains" of your raw materials, be they animal, vegetable, or mineral? And are there strains that you are neglecting because they seem too difficult or too demanding to develop? Like our cacao, these new strains may offer an unexpected benefit, increasing resiliency in the face of disruptions or developments in the future.

A CHOCOLATE LOVER'S RESPONSIBILITY

There is one final thing to consider when you look at chocolate production, and that's the way those who do the hard, backbreaking work of growing the beans themselves are treated. I believe in transparency. I travel as often as I can to the plantations that grow our beans. I talk (through interpreters) to anyone I can. I look to see if the workers seem well and happy. But we are anomalies.

Too often, especially in cacao production, the growers themselves are treated terribly and receive far too little payment for their products. These rock-bottom prices are passed on to the consumer, which explains why you can purchase a generic chocolate bar for less than a dollar or a euro. These farmers universally grow the Forastero bean—hardy, robust, but very low quality. When prices go up, vast acres of forest in West Africa are cleared overnight by small-scale subsistence farmers who often lack the trucks, roads, and other infrastructure to get their beans to market. As a result, the beans pass through a complex series of buyers, agents, and intermediaries before finally being purchased by companies whose names are familiar to us all.

This tangled web of middlemen separates the farmers from the conglomerates who ultimately purchase their products. The former lose all bargaining power because they are never in direct contact with the people who are actually purchasing their product, or indeed with other farmers. The large conglomerates are able to claim plausible deniability about the conditions in which these farmers live and grow, because it inevitably becomes almost impossible to say where exactly they are purchasing the beans from. Even when the governments of these countries get involved, as did Ivory Coast and Ghana, it backfires: prices go up high enough so that more farmers enter the market, which depresses the prices all over again. Either way, the farmers remain mired in poverty. In desperation they resort to clearing more forest and planting more cacao in a monoculture of Forastero beans. The lack of shade and deep roots speeds up the degradation of the soil, and the lack of biodiversity kills insect and animal life. Eventually, the soil is drained of life, and the farmers move deeper into the forest, clearing new land on which to grow their crop.

Meanwhile, the Forastero beans are fermented and dried in Africa, and then shipped to brands all across the world, where they are processed for seventy-two hours at near boiling temperatures, getting rid of the volatile acidity and off flavors of the Forastero. Of course, whatever good flavors the bean might have had are also lost in the process. So, as a final step, various flavorings including artificial vanilla, known as vanillin[1] (made of various ingredients, most notably a by-product left after extracting cellulose from wood for paper-making), are added. Many more fashionable, "higher quality" brands are doing a similar thing, adding increasingly daring and even provocative flavors that overwhelm the actual (bad) taste of the chocolate (sometimes mass-produced chocolate that is melted down, flavored, and disguised as better quality "hipster" bars, sold at similar prices to our own bars).

Many months after harvesting, the chocolate finally makes its way to the shelves. It is sold as bars or hot chocolate or as Easter eggs, chocolate chips, chocolate milk, ice cream, or other desserts. And we all (even me at times) pick a few items here or there to satisfy our sweet tooth or please our children. I'd encourage anyone reading this to think a little more about the origins of this very inexpensive chocolate. Hidden behind the packaging is an untold story of the suffering of millions of people, working in desperate poverty, and corporations that have little accountability toward them. Many of these farmers have never even tasted chocolate themselves. It is simply something that is either not available where they live or is priced too high for them to afford.

This is not how we wish to do business, both for practical reasons (we want the best quality of bean to create the very best chocolate) and the obvious moral ones. Very early on with Domori we realized that our growers did not eat or enjoy chocolate. This disconnect made it hard to communicate with them about what was working and what wasn't. Rather than attempt to change growers, we decided to educate and involve them in the final product. Every time a grower sends a sample of their new production to Domori, we make sure to send boxes of chocolate back to the plantations that grew the beans. I encourage everyone to taste the different bars of chocolate. Then, when a coworker or I return, we are sharing a common language with the men and women who pick and process our raw materials. I can explain how important it is for the quality of the chocolate that cacao is properly fermented and dried in the shade because, otherwise, the final taste will have a bitterness to it or some off-flavors. Since we now have a shared reference, they understand exactly what I'm talking about.

Other plantations might not treat growers so poorly, but still show a lack of care or attention. The vines or trees are unevenly watered, shedding leaves through lack of care. The fast-growing vines are not properly pruned, and in the worst case you might see the remnant of a worker's lunch, left like litter in a shady spot. These kinds of signs are clear warnings to me. They tell me that there is a lack of care that will result in a lack of quality. The best growers love their work and their plantations; they want everything to be perfect. These are the people we want to be in business with.

MANCINI AND ITALIAN CULTIVATION

It takes many long flights and arduous hours of connections to return home to Trieste from the Quito, Ecuador, airport. By the time I finally open my door and am greeted by my wife, I am exhausted and hungry. All I wish is for a simple bowl of pasta and a glass of good wine. The latter varies, but the former is always Mancini pasta, a small, artisanal brand of exceptional quality. My wife boils a pot of spaghetti and quickly makes a simple tomato and basil sauce. The pasta is roughly textured rather than the smooth, industrial pasta most of us are used to. The sauce clings to it. The whole dish is delicious. It reminds me of all the reasons I am so happy to be home.

Massimo Mancini truly loves his pasta. As a young man, he decided to take over his grandfather's old farm, build a small factory, and create a "vertical" pasta company. From the wheat to the final product, everything would be done on their property, by them. Pasta is a staple in Italy, where 63 percent[2] of Italians eat it every day. Yet, as Massimo Mancini points out, 98 percent of the pasta sold is what we would consider industrially produced (Barilla, in its famous blue box, is the most popular brand). It is such an everyday part of our lives that few of us ask about what goes into our pasta, or where those raw materials come from. However, any product and crop (in this case wheat) that is ubiquitous has a huge effect, both on the land on which it is grown and the people who tend to it and eventually eat it.

As Mancini moves forward with growing his business, he faces three cultivation challenges. First, growing the high-quality wheat he requires to make his pasta in a sustainable way; second, producing the pasta in a way that can eventually scale up; and third, persuading Italians and the world of the unique quality of his older, slower methods.

Like our cacao plantations and the multiple strains of Criollo we nurture and tend to, Mancini grows multiple strains of wheat: Maestà, Nazareno, and now Nonno Mariano, a variety of wheat they developed and named after his beloved grandfather. They take great care to plant each strain of wheat in an optimal location, and they wait longer than most growers to harvest, so there's less humidity in the grains. The crops absorb water that comes directly from the soil and the atmosphere. The water used in the dough comes directly from the Sibillini Mountains. Every step Mancini takes adds more work to what they do, and every step is in alignment with GAP, or Good Agricultural Practices.

FUTUREPROOFING

This work leads to better pasta, but it's also an essential part of trying to build resilience into the future of all crops. We are constantly looking at ways to futureproof our cacao, grapes, and tea. For Mancini, it is wheat. A 2016 study found that wheat[3] production will decline by 4.6 percent with a 1°C rise in global temperatures. Wheat production also leads to fertilizer runoff that causes algae blooms in rivers, lakes, and eventually the ocean. The resulting hypoxia harms sea life and contributes to the ongoing degradation of the environment.

When I talk with Massimo Mancini about this, he says, "You cannot put wheat after wheat on the same ground, every year. It exploits the soil. Instead, rotation is the first principle. That's why out of six hundred hectares of fields, only half is planted with durum wheat at any one time. The other half is for pulses like alfalfa, clover, fava beans, pea beans or chickpeas, or industrial crops like rapeseed or sunflowers. These crops give back nitrogen to the soil. We do regular analysis of the soil and the fields to know exactly the property of the fields. From this, we can choose which varieties of wheat to plant, where, and how to tend to them." Mancini chose not to be certified 100 percent organic, but the Good Agricultural Practice has allowed them to meet the zero-residue threshold on their crops anyway. They are demonstrating a way to thoughtfully and rigorously ensure that their crops have resiliency moving forward.

Part of cultivation is having this kind of awareness of what the future will bring, and how to prepare for it. Unsurprisingly, it is small producers like Mancini who are at the forefront of this kind of preparation. Most pasta manufacturers in Italy do not grow their own wheat; they buy it as a commodity from large growers and sellers instead. In Mancini's own region, he is one of a handful of farmers not selling to a large, industrial conglomerate (Carlo Latini is another). He is also one of the very few pasta makers still using old-fashioned bronze dies, rather than modern Teflon dies, to shape his pasta. When we talk, he explains why he embraced such old-fashioned technology. "The industrial pasta's surface is very smooth because the industrial companies use Teflon dies to shape their pasta," he tells me. "They produce six or seven times more pasta per hour, but the surface will be smooth and the pasta won't keep the sauce. We use the bronze dies, so we produce very slowly. But if you use the bronze ones, you obtain this kind of spaghetti, with a very rough surface that is able to keep the sauce in the best way."

Mancini's product is superb. There is a potentially unlimited market for what he does. Yet the very thing that makes his pasta so great—his control over the wheat, his care and thought about growing it, his refusal to buy wheat from other growers—ensures that it will be a slow process to expand.

Massimo tells me how the biggest problem is that most people do not fully understand the culture of semolina pasta. Consumers generally consider pasta *porta sugo*, or a sauce vehicle. Italians each eat fifty-seven pounds of pasta per year on average. But if you ask, "What do you know about this pasta—do you know about this variety?" they scratch their heads. "When I started ten years ago," says Massimo, "I went to meet the chefs, the delis, but they all sold Barilla, De Cecco. I absolutely respect these brands, but 99 percent of pasta is industrial. We try to speak about our fields, our method."

Like Domori, where we must work to educate our customers about our product, so, too, must Mancini continue to educate *his* customers about what a great pasta is, and why it is worth paying a little more for something that elevates a meal in the way his product does. This is the final facet of cultivation, the ongoing development of a customer who understands and appreciates the extra depth of quality that Mancini offers.

EIGHT

REFINEMENT

Augmented quality, the cornerstone of Incanto, requires one to go further in pursuit of perfection. It isn't hard to make a good product, but it is the final stages of refinement that make a great product. Refinement is quite simply the ongoing process of improving what you do over time. Refinement happens in two different ways: first, through continuous improvements in the production process. This is the world of innovations and improvements, new ideas, techniques, and philosophies that propel us further and further into the future. These could be ways to improve your product, your distribution, or your communication and engagement with your customers.

The second way of refinement is almost the opposite. Instead of moving forward, it requires staying still or even moving backward, adopting and following the ancient traditions your ancestors established before there was refrigeration or electrical power. Allowing the processes of smoking, fermentation, or salting (all of which take months, years, or even decades) can elevate your product from good to extraordinary. For this chapter, we will look at the most refined of all products: great wine.

On the Karst Plateau surrounding Trieste, 1,300 feet above sea level, are wineries that Luigi Veronelli, the "father" of top-quality wine production in Italy, would call *heroic*. They persist despite the bracing Bora, lashing the land with gusts of wind so strong you fear they will knock you over. Vineyards grow determinedly in the poor, stony soil, blended with clay, persisting despite the lack of water. One of these heroic vintners, Vodopivec (ironically, a name that means "drink water" in the Slovenian language), produces wines from the local white grape called Vitovska, a varietal that thrives in the harsh conditions.

Paolo Vodopivec follows the ancient process of fermenting the grapes with the skins (nowadays the juice of white grapes is first separated from the skins) and, when the wine is ready, ages it in amphoras buried underground. It's a sophisticated system of vinification, coming from Georgia where they have produced wines since the Neolithic age; the amphoras protect the wine from oxidation without the need for additives, leaving a cleaner and mineral-tasting wine. The aging will last for some years and, after bottling, this white wine (which Americans would call *orange*, as in a white wine that is made with extended skin contact) will last like a red one. For Vodopivec and other vintners adopting the ancient technology of amphoras, moving forward and refining what they do actually meant moving backward to adopt ancient methods and old ways of doing things.

I often bike past the winery on a pleasant weekend afternoon, first pedaling past the flower farm he also runs. Paolo Vodopivec himself is famously media shy. In one of his few interviews, he explained that skin contact is "an instrument to allow me to express the grape."[1] Here is both the promise and challenge of refinement: Italian growers and producers pursue refinement in part because it requires (or allows) one to adapt to the peculiarities of one's land and available raw materials.

Say a thousand years ago you had a herd of Orobica goats, famous for their towering horns and soft, lustrous hair. If you also had a high alpine climate and mountain biodiversity, you might end up with a hard cheese like Bitto, created in the Valtellina Mountains of Lombardy. The cows, goats, and sheep that are milked for this cheese are kept in high altitudes during summer. As a result, Bitto has a distinctive herbaceous taste that subtly changes to reflect the differing sweetness and tastes of the grasses where the animals grazed during the particular day they were milked. There is no written recipe. Most of the shepherds and cheesemakers who produce it sell out before it is officially for sale.[2]

Even if you wanted to replicate Bitto, you couldn't. One valley over and the cheese would be completely different, reflecting the nuances of a subtly different microclimate and culture. It is in your interest to make the very best cheese you can with the resources available to you. It is also in your interest to embrace those things that make your product unique, even when they may limit production or cap your revenue at a certain level.

You will find producers who embrace this philosophy all over Italy. They understand that well-aged wine, cheese, or ham requires a unique and perfect environment, time, and the experience to detect when it goes from good to exceptional. They intuitively embrace the quirks of climate, culture, and raw materials that shape their products. We have about five hundred varieties of cheeses in Italy, many of them granted "protected status" by the European Commission. An even smaller number are "DOP" or Denominazione di Origine Protetta (translated as "Protected Designation of Origin"[3]). This designation is a guarantee to the consumer that the cheese was made locally, using traditional methods. A DOP balsamic vinegar from Reggio Emilia or Modena requires an astonishing amount of labor. Unlike red or white wine vinegar, the grape juice is not fermented into wine first. Instead, the whole grape, including skin, stems, and seeds, is pressed and boiled down into a "must." The process usually uses Trebbiano di Castelvetro, which is white and often surprises people who expect a red or purple grape.

This is slowly boiled down until it is half the original amount of juice. Now the must ferments, evolving the taste from the fresh sweetness of grape juice into the sharp yet sweet, distinctive tang of truly extraordinary balsamic vinegar. The must is stored in barrels that have been rinsed with boiling vinegar. It ages for a year, when the thick, sweet liquid is transferred into a series of wooden kegs (each one smaller than the last) known as *batterie*. A *batteria* can be made of various woods such as ash, mulberry, juniper, cherry, chestnut, acacia, or oak. Like a fine wine, the vinegar eventually takes on the subtle notes of the wood, even as it evaporates, further condensing and intensifying the liquid.[4] All the while a tester, or *acetaio*, samples the evolving vinegar. At some point between twelve and thirty-five years later, the *acetaio* deems it ready to be bottled and sold, and the individual bottles are sealed with a foil cap whose color denotes approximately how old the vinegar is.[5]

This process doesn't account for the endless rows of balsamic vinegar that line supermarket shelves and sell for a few euros, pounds, or dollars. Those vinegars are more likely a blend of concentrated vinegar and juice, aged for a few years, and sold without any great concern for a more refined taste.

Worse, some truly low-end balsamic vinegars are "faked" with grape juice, sugar, and artificial flavors to mimic the notes of wood found in authentic DOP vinegar.

Sometimes refinement is as simple as closing a door, walking away, and leaving the finished product at the right temperature and humidity in a warehouse. Likewise, our parmigiano cheeses are sold at different levels of aging (from twelve up to seventy-nine months), and the San Daniele ham is aged for a minimum of thirteen to thirty-six months. Of course, this isn't cheap or easy. Refinement always requires two things: superb raw materials, sourced from very precise areas; and human labor at every step, including those that less refined brands long ago mechanized.

San Marzano tomatoes are picked by hand, out of the volcanic soil laid down millennia ago by Mount Vesuvius and the slumbering supervolcano Campi Flegrei in the Valle del Sarno, near Naples. A can of authentic San Marzanos can cost four or five times that of the "San Marzano-style" tomatoes sold by American farmers. It is possible to plant the seeds, but even the most industrious Midwesterner cannot replicate the layers of ancient volcanic ash, the rich minerals of which create a sweeter, less acidic fruit. Nor can they afford to gently harvest and peel them by hand, preserving the cylindrical shape, rather than processing them into a diced or pureed product preferred by American consumers.

This trade-off is worth it for the Italian farmers who have grown this fruit for generations. Their tomatoes are layered with meaning and tradition, and they have become an essential raw material for other businesses' Incanto products. Their value and desirability make them an essential ingredient for many classic Italian dishes, none more so than *pizza napoletana*. Naples has some of the very best pizza in Italy, even having an official body—Associazione Verace Pizza

Napoletana—that dictates how real Neapolitan pizza is prepared. San Marzanos are one of only three acceptable options, all sourced from the area immediately around Naples.[6]

THE REFINEMENT PARADOX

Businesses that produce these kinds of high-quality, but relatively common raw materials have a choice: either pursue an elevated and refined product or maximize output to take advantage of the more price-conscious marketplace. My choice will always be to pursue the highest quality possible. Yes, a single-minded dedication to refinement will limit the amount of product you can produce. There will be millions of potential customers you will never be able to reach. But the customers you *can* reach will not balk at the price you must charge, understanding that this is a trade-off for superb, augmented quality. Likewise, those who purchase your products as a raw material will integrate them into their own products, relying on you to supply augmented quality on which they can build.

It pains me that this lesson has not been fully learned yet. I have had the frequent experience of ordering a steak in America, and finding the taste very good, but the meat too hard. It has not been allowed to age the way it would in Italy, where we accept that it must hang for weeks before it will be suitable for cooking and serving. Hanging meat, or fermenting for decades, or allowing a cheese to mature for years in a dark cave, is a choice. Perhaps you choose to shave a few years or months off of the process, rushing your product to market in the name of efficiency and profitability. There are plenty of potential customers who will not understand that the product they are buying was denied that final layer of refinement. You will most likely still have buyers. Yet you will not have the satisfaction of creating something so superb it lingers for years afterward in the memory of all who try it.

Even more important, you will not inspire the devotion of customers who remember the unparalleled quality of your product years after first trying it.

ILLY REFINEMENT

If you cannot turn to the past to refine your product, turn to the future. In the 1970s, my father, Ernesto, realized that the single serving "pod" style of coffee was the future of our industry. He was quite literally years ahead of the competition in realizing this. He dedicated years to perfecting this process, looking for every opportunity to offer a refined and superior product in a category that generally prioritizes speed and efficiency over excellence. Here's another element of refinement: you need to look hard to find those areas where there is room to improve. What have you not yet tried?

One key element in determining the quality of espresso is the degree of grinding. If it's too coarse, the espresso will be weak. If it's too fine, the espresso will be bitter and astringent. We had a tradition at illy then: a worker whose primary job was to hand-check the degree of grinding in the production line. He would wander the line, using his eye to determine which grinds to check, then scoop up a small amount of coffee and prepare a cup of espresso. If the espresso brewed in a precise amount of time (generally twenty to thirty seconds), then the grind was correct. The shorter the time, the coarser the grinding; the longer the time, the finer the grinding.

My father wanted to refine this process, using modern technology to ensure a truly uniform and precise grind. One day he was idly reading a scientific magazine when he stumbled upon an article about lasers. It described how one could detect the precise degree of a ground powder's fineness by using a laser. A computer would detect the diffraction of the laser ray caused by the ground particles crossing it and calculate a figure. Ernesto immediately realized the potential for his own company. Instead of nondescript particles, he would use the laser to check the coffee grinds, guaranteeing his customers the perfect degree of grinding to brew a rich, smooth espresso.

In the end, to my eternal sadness, my father's vision was still not enough to elevate our pod system ahead of our megacompetitors. Our pods, even the very basic, early model, undoubtedly produced better coffee, partly because of the superior nature of the coffee itself, partly because of the way the water ran more slowly through the pod, and partly because of the fine grind of the coffee. What's more, our pods, due to their paper construction, were universal. Customers could use them in any ESE (easy serving espresso) machine. We promoted the incorporation of the ESE Consortium inspired by the case history of VHS vs. Betamax videotapes; the first was an open system, the second (promoted by Sony) a closed one. The huge coffee conglomerates that arrived later had the power of scale to impose their capsule. Nonetheless, the ESE system is still on the market, appreciated for its quality and respect of the environment.

GENERATIONAL REFINEMENT

Peter Drucker often wrote that one should consider profits to be at least partially an investment in your business's future. He meant that before satisfying the shareholders, profits are needed to maintain the competitiveness of the company over time. Thanks to accelerating and diffused technological progress, new and better products are brought to the market. If your company won't improve its production, sooner or later, it will be beaten by competitors.

After our competitor changed the coffee paradigm with its capsule system, we decided to make our own closed system, and spent years in research and development. Eventually, we devised the illy capsules, which have five unique patents. It's the sole capsule that hasn't been cloned or copied. This may be because it has two main refinements over earlier versions of the pod. The first is a membrane that facilitates the emulsion between oils and water: The more oils that are emulsified, the more flavors will be in the cup. The more emulsified oils you have in the cup, then the thicker and longer lasting the crema that floats atop the espresso. Have you ever ordered an espresso at the end of a delightful meal in a good restaurant, only to find that it arrives with the crema "shattered" or broken, and the dark brown of the coffee is slowly drowning it? This signifies that the coffee is already past its peak moment of perfection. Though customers might not realize this, intuitively they understand that the coffee is not quite as good as it could have been. They drink it, enjoying the taste, but wondering how that taste might have been better.

The second refinement is that the capsule is put in a filter holder that conveys the espresso into the cup with no contact between the machine and the coffee. Because the coffee never touches the machine, leaving deposits and bad flavors, you do not have to clean it.

These are subtle refinements, but they took years to develop. Only someone who is truly committed to quality would have prioritized years of research and development to protect the crema or limit the chance of contaminating a new coffee with the taste of an old one.

At Mastrojanni, we were quite satisfied with the quality of our wines. When it came time to enlarge the cellar, my nephew, Ernesto, who is an architect, suggested building it based on bioarchitectural principles. His project did not use concrete or contain steel, just bricks, wood, and stones. He thought that steel affects or might create magnetic fields, which in turn endanger the health of human beings. Perhaps, he thought, they might affect the quality of our Brunello, which stays in the cellar for at least three years. No steel and no magnetic fields mean no bad influence on the quality of the wines. We now compensate for humidity, temperature, and magnetic fields in our cellars, and we believe the quality of our Brunello di Montalcino is improved by the lack of magnetic fields.

Refinement is a constant process of trying one thing and then another. I do not know for certain that the magnetic fields were negatively affecting our wine. However, this is part of the process of always pushing to perfect and improve what you do. Likewise, these types of refinements are part of the ongoing process of finding some small space where you can move ahead of your rivals in terms of quality. The other wineries may scoff at our innovations, and perhaps they are right. Yet, if we are right, we will have a dramatic improvement that they cannot emulate, perhaps for years.

ORNELLAIA

There are literally thousands of artisanal food businesses in Italy, creating excellent wines and cheeses and vinegars and meats. Some have a national name, but many of them are so local that they sell their products only within their own towns. These obscure foods are loved because they are so specific to a region. Nothing tastes of home quite as much as a cheese that is only available there. However, there are other ways to add a level of refinement for your product.

The Ornellaia winery is unlike the other examples in this chapter. For one, though the estate is owned by an old family with deep roots and traditions in winemaking, the Frescobaldis, the actual estate is young, founded in 1981. And rather than being based in a region with a strong and deep-rooted tradition of wine, they are attempting something new, by growing wine in an area that until relatively recently wasn't considered a wine region. Part of this stems from a very Italian kind of snobbery: for centuries, most people in Tuscany believed that Sangiovese was wine and wine was Sangiovese. If you couldn't make any good Sangiovese, you couldn't make good wine. Ornellaia is dedicated to producing charming and uplifting wines full of subtle flavors and finesse to express the unique terroir in Bolgheri on the Tuscan coast.

To understand how bold it is for Ornellaia to plant anything other than Sangioveses on their vineyards, first you have to understand what Sangiovese means to Tuscan winemaking. Sangiovese has deep roots, first grown by our forebears, the Etruscans. Some believe the name derives from the Latin *sanguis Jovis*, or "the blood of Jupiter." Sangiovese also makes up the bulk of the blended Chianti wines, whose classic straw-wrapped *fiasco* bottles helped popularize relatively inexpensive Italian wine around the world. So, when Ornellaia was founded in an area where it was commonly understood that you couldn't grow this quintessentially Italian grape, they had to take a chance and do something new.

Today their winery, neatly wedged in the low hills of Bolgheri, is planted with multiple different vineyards, each with a distinctive soil: deep, graveled clay perhaps, or a mix of sand and clay. During the heat of a Tuscan summer, the nearby Tyrrhenian Sea prevents the temperatures from reaching extremes, instead staying cool at night, which is necessary for a slow and flavorful ripening. The vines are densely planted to force them to compete against one another for nutrients and hydration. This forces the plant to grow fewer, more densely concentrated grapes. The grapes, which include Petit Verdot, Cabernet Sauvignon, or Merlot, are picked specifically for these small parcels of land and their varied terroir. Their single vineyard, Masseto Merlot, born on the estate but now a separate entity, is considered one of the world's finest Merlots and has sold at more than $1,000 a bottle at auction.

REFINEMENT: OLD AND NEW

Ornellaia moves forward toward refinement with its collaborations with contemporary artists (more on this in a moment) and simultaneously moves "back" to older, less technical ways of producing grapes. In Tuscany, the average hours per year worked in a vineyard per hectare is 245. The average hours that Ornellaia works on its vineyards is 623. This means more dedication to quality. This means that they do not perform any mechanized activity on the vineyards. Instead, everything is done by hand. If you do everything by hand, you can pay more attention and give more care, so the final products are obviously of higher quality. This insistence on doing things by hand and understanding the nuance of the winery's every varietal pays off in the next stage: the blend. This is something I come to see and understand when I get a chance to visit the winery myself.

I visited the Ornellaia winery on a warm, sunny day in June, and was given a tour by the area manager for Europe, Matteo

Zanardello. I was immediately impressed by the air of calm and harmony. The winery is surrounded by a wood on one side, vineyards on the other.

After my tour, we sat for an hour, sampling the different wines and enjoying the golden light of early evening as the sun set over the hills that sat between us and the Mediterranean. Matteo Zanardello tells me that they produce five wines out of 115 hectares, all of which are blends. The first is for Ornellaia, the estate's flagship wine. Then Le Serre Nuove dell'Ornellaia, the estate's second wine.

This blending is the art, the refinement. The winemaker tastes up to ninety different wines, each barreled separately, unblended, so that a year later, when it is time to create the wines, he has a full palette to pull from. This is not easy. This is the artistic side of wine production. There is no scientific metric that would determine the blend. Instead, it's all about feelings, sensations, and knowing how you want the wine to taste in the future. As we talk, I sense the family's appreciation and awe at the skill of their winemaker. Simply tasting that many raw, unblended wines with strong tannins and undeveloped flavors would be overpowering for most people. Yet the winemaker, with his artist's vision of what might come out of these raw materials, is undeterred.

The end result is a kind of relaxed quality: Ornellaia does not position itself as "luxury" despite the excellence of its wines. Instead, its mission is to be recognized for world-class wines from Bolgheri on the Tuscan coast. This idea, that there is a difference between luxury and superb quality, is an interesting one. To me it suggests that when pursuing Incanto, you should always focus on the actual product you are making, rather than the way the product is received or promoted in the marketplace. There are plenty of "luxury" goods that the cognoscenti know to avoid, preferring instead less well-known but superior brands. And, indeed, Ornellaia *is* the epitome of refined good taste and style. It has even partnered to open a restaurant in Zurich that is the height of refined, minimalist chic.

CREATIVE REFINEMENT

It's easy to pursue and develop a refined product when you have hundreds of years of history and tradition to pull from. When you don't, as with Ornellaia, you have to get creative with those added refinements.

One issue for any winery is how you communicate a difference between this vintage and the previous one. You want to engage your audience every year. And it's difficult to engage your audience every year because only wine collectors and wine lovers will understand the differences between two different vintages. As Matteo says, "If we talk about that, then we are just talking to a very narrow audience. So, we needed a way to engage the audience by talking about our wine and giving a different side to our estate."

Ornellaia has solved this conundrum in a unique way: each of its vintages is different, and the difference is celebrated by assigning a word that describes the character of every vintage. The practice began in 2006 when the vintage was very exuberant, so it was *L'Esuberanza*. The word was given to an artist who produced a limited edition of large-format bottles, a label for the 750-ml bottle of Ornellaia, and site-specific artwork for the estate.

Every year starts from the wine. Each of these words goes back to the vintage that emerged. For example, *L'Eleganza* in 2013: there was more Merlot in the blend of Ornellaia, and the end result was a more elegant wine. To celebrate

L'Eleganza, Ornellaia commissioned the Japanese artist Yutaka Sone to make a project specifically for the blend. The 2014 vintage was more difficult and challenging. The weather had been cool and rainy; everyone had to work harder to reap a good harvest. The end result was the very core of the estate, a limited amount of wine that revealed the heart of the winery, or its *L'Essenza.*

And this is the final way to add refinement to your product: find a way to make it unique, essential. Add a layer of story or communication that reveals both the joy of your work (*L'Esuberanza*) and the occasional heartache and struggle (*L'Essenza*). Ornellaia's strategy to share some truth about the wine, and some small insight into the heart of the people who make it, creates a compelling reason for people who like the wine to learn to love it.

NINE

RELATIONSHIPS

I n the spring, when it is neither too hot nor too rainy, I love to ride my BMW R 1200 GS through the mountains of the Alps surrounding Trieste. Immersing myself in the natural landscape can be a kind of meditation, taking me momentarily out of the stress of running Polo del Gusto. And, of course, no one can call or email or text, just for those few minutes, racing through the oak and the pine forests high above the coast. Recently, I arrived home from such a ride. As I took off my helmet, the cell phone started ringing. I answered with my ears still disturbed by the rush of the wind. Instead of announcing his name, the person calling asked, "Who am I?" It took me only a second to recognize the voice of a customer in the Tuscany region whom I had visited a few weeks earlier. So, I answered by saying his name, fortunately the right one.

For him it was absolutely normal that I identified his voice among hundreds of customers and after several weeks' time; for me it was an interesting challenge. Also an important one. All our professional relationships are personal. Our products impress our customers, but it is the relationship between us that cements a onetime sale into a long-term business. Building and developing this relationship was simpler when business was mostly personal and on the phone. Email and texts are no substitute for the immediacy of a personal conversation. Today I travel more, not less, despite these advancements in technology. Face-to-face is still the best way to nourish your relationships with the people who actually buy your products. When I'm not visiting these *pasticcerie*, wine distributors, and gelato makers, I'm making and preserving these relationships at fairs, exhibitions, and conventions.

BUILDING RELATIONSHIPS WITH YOUR CUSTOMERS

Building and maintaining relationships with your customers is more challenging now, in the era of lockdowns and quarantines, than it was before. At Polo del Gusto, we are organizing professional courses for pastry chefs and other craftsmen, emailing continuously to keep all the customers posted with the latest information, and communicating daily through social media.

One advantage of a business with a strong sense of heritage and a love of authenticity is that your story is ongoing, even as the media you use changes: digital instead of billboards, podcast sponsorships instead of radio. But you can continue to tell the same story. Indeed, now, when the world is in flux and your competitors may be reacting impulsively to every change in the weather, you can cement your place in your customers' awareness by being consistent and leaning into that history. For illy, our story is partly visual: we have a clean, simple logo that all Italians see every day as they order espresso on their way to work. This story is a kind of glue between you and your customer. Our cups literally feel different in the hand from any other espresso cup. The handle sits a little higher so that the balance of the cup is unlike others. For any Italian who grew up holding this cup every day, there is a neurological shortcut in their brain (also known as a heuristic). illy = coffee and, more important, illy = *my* coffee. All of our advertising points in the same direction, reminding our customers that they grew up drinking our coffee. Not only that, but they also grew up watching their mothers and grandmothers save our tins, using them to store other kitchen goods or perhaps sewing supplies or spare items on a hallway desk. Now they do the same. For them, the taste, sight, sound, and smell of illy equals home.

These shortcuts in the brain and emotional links between your customer and your product are part of your relationship with the people who love what you make and regularly buy it. Every time a customer holds a cup, or saves an illy can, it puts another brick in the structure of that relationship, and those mental links grow stronger. If you don't know what your brand's version of the cup or the can is, then it is important to find it. What is the link between your product and your customer? And, more important, if you aren't telling a clear story about your product, what story are your current or potential customers telling themselves about your brand? Customers don't lose themselves. Poor products and bad branding lose them instead.

As you move forward, you can add new chapters to the story, always maintaining its basic pillars. The same should be made, in my opinion, through advertising, perhaps changing some of the details of your images or slogans, but always staying true to the core of your product or brand. Once you find an advertising campaign that works, and that uniquely communicates the message of your company, you should keep on it. We have found that advertising agencies are often keen to "try something new." Perhaps people within your own organization are recommending a big relaunch or rebrand. Unless your old strategy is so bad that your company is in imminent peril of failing, I'd suggest that, rather than starting from scratch, you try to refine the branding materials you already have.

I had my own experience of the peril of "change for change's sake" when I was the governor (*presidente* in Italian) for the Region Friuli Venezia Giulia (the area that Trieste is in). Our advertising slogan was loosely translated as, "Be a guest of unique people." In our region there are three living linguistic minorities protected by the national and regional laws. These different cultures mean we have different foods, traditions, and ways of living, all of which are charming and appealing to tourists. There is nowhere else in Italy like it. However, when I stepped down after five years, the new governor changed it. Now our slogan is: "Friuli Venezia Giulia . . . with open arms." A claim that could be used by any region in the world.

Not only was this a case of changing something that didn't need to be changed, but it was a case of ignoring an established story that was specific to the "product," and replacing it with something so generic that it had little chance of creating a mental shortcut in the potential customer's brain. There will always be people within an organization who don't like the elements of your business that are unique to you (I'm sure we have people at illy who think the logo could be updated, or the cups refined). This is okay. Not everyone has to love everything.

BUILDING RELATIONSHIPS WITH YOUR EMPLOYEES

Everything I know about building relationships in business I learned from my father, Ernesto, watching as he negotiated every conceivable challenge at work. My father's key word was *respect.* He was respectful to his customers, to his suppliers, and most of all to his employees. He didn't care what their role was within the company, or what their social position was outside of it. He was a man of his generation, with a certain old-world formality to his manners. Yet he knew how to be friendly and familiar with the people who worked for him, perhaps adding in a dash of formality depending on the nature of the relationship and the time passed since he first met the person. He had an almost magical way of putting people at ease. Blue-collar workers felt they could talk to him and be honest about their work. In another country or another type of company, these workers might not feel so emboldened to talk frankly. British heavy manufacturing, for instance, collapsed for multiple reasons. But the decline was exacerbated by distrust between workers and management. One (possibly apocryphal) story is of a factory where the workers went on strike often. Each time they did, the owner bought a new Rolls-Royce, which he would drive by the picket lines, making a rude sign with his hands out the window.[1]

I learned from my father to treat other people as I want to be treated and to talk easily and broadly on subjects that are not necessarily related to the work. My father knew that personal and familiar matters are important for building good relationships. He understood that work doesn't exist distinct from an employee's home life. When an individual had to tend to a sick relative, he didn't chastise them for going home. Part of this dynamic stems from something we mentioned earlier: working for my father was a good job. Our employees were likewise respectful of us because they knew they were well treated. They wanted to remain at illy as much as we wanted to keep them. And together, we worked to create a company that was beneficial to the town. Part of this is environmental sustainability. Part of it is supporting our employees as they put down roots, bought homes, and educated their children.

We mentioned in chapter 7, "Cultivation," how workers and small farmers in Central and South America, West Africa, the Caribbean, and India are often grossly abused and underpaid (or not paid at all). Farmers often sell at a loss rather than a profit. The excellent raw material we buy from these countries is rare and costs much more than the commodities traded at the New York Stock Exchange. For instance, Forastero cacao is traded at the NYSE at about $2,500 per ton, and we pay about four times this price for Criollo. We buy directly from the growers, not only to nurture a relationship that allows continuous improvements of the production, but also to leave the whole margin to the grower. illy's supply chain is certified for its sustainability by DNV (Det Norske Veritas), which checks that our claims correspond to the price paid to the growers. Part of the concept of relationship is ensuring that we treat our suppliers well and give our customers a good reason to spend more for more ethical products. By refining our produce to ever higher quality, we do just that.

ROBUSTO TIES

B Corporations, which are established both for purpose and profit, are increasingly in vogue (illy recently completed its certification process). However, I'd argue that most family-run businesses in Italy espouse the B Corp ethos. Here, the concept of a company that equally prioritizes purpose and profit finds a fertile habitat. Family-run companies, even ones that have grown to become medium-sized or global enterprises, maintain the familiar approach. Even when run by professional boards and managers, they consider the employees like members of the enlarged family. The relationships are not only good, but often friendly; if employees need help, the company will help them, and when the company needs help, in tough times such as the pandemic, the employee will help the company.

Think of the way we treat our employees as "robusto ties," a variation of the strong and weak tie concept. Strong ties are your immediate family and the people you know closely and deeply. Weak ties are more superficial, but essential for a smoothly operating society. This describes the connection between a child and a friendly neighbor who will watch over the child if their parents work late, or an overworked parent and a helpful café waitress who remembers their order. A weak tie at work is generally a casual connection; perhaps someone in a different department whom you know superficially, but who can provide an introduction to someone else in that department. Robusto ties are somewhere between the two: I do not know all my employees deeply, but our relationship is more than strictly professional and transactional. We are like distant members of the same family, tied together by history, culture, and a shared interest in the success of our business. We may not be directly involved in each other's lives, but when our family is threatened we will pull together and fight for it. Likewise, when times are good, we will all share in the benefits.

We have many employees who work for us for their entire career. Eventually, when it comes close to retirement, they begin to introduce the idea of passing on their job to their children. Their position becomes an intergenerational job. This works for them in that they can help their children to get established at a good company. It works for us in that it helps us to nurture a tight and friendly environment full of the robusto ties[2] that help to keep a group or organization together. By hiring within the same family, we reduce the risk of hiring a person of bad character or poor ethics. We know their parents and have often met the children many times over the course of their youth, even while they were still in school. Like Luigi Biasetto suggests, we often know their grandparents too. We understand the environment in which these young people have been raised and we can feel confident of how they will behave when working for us. There is another benefit for me: I don't enjoy firing people and would rather take extra care in hiring the right ones. In most B companies, "firing" is considered a painful act; there are entrepreneurs who decide to cut their own compensation rather than fire some employees.

THE GOOD JOB

All of this is partly because Italy is a family-oriented country, and we prioritize the happiness of those in our immediate and extended orbit. However, it is also a practical choice. We in Italy have a volatile past. In Trieste we have belonged to numerous other countries, been fought over, and had to defend our territory many times. We have lived through political turmoil; we had a viable Communist party even up to the 1990s. We have always lived with the possibility of political uncertainty, strife, and even extremism. So, we create stability where we can. It is worth it to make a little less profit if our company has happier employees. Not simply for "feel good" reasons, but because this makes us more resilient, stronger, and more likely to survive in difficult times. The year 2020 was challenging for us, as with many food and coffee companies. People were no longer going to the cafés that sell our products. Our supply chains struggled in places as their employees fell ill. Yet, throughout all of this, I felt confident that our employees in all branches of Polo del Gusto were as supportive of us as we were of them.

(Interestingly, Domori was the most resilient company during the pandemic. The management strived to find new opportunities to sell: new markets, new products, new customers. At the end of the year, the sales were almost as high as the previous year's numbers. When the pandemic hit, we expected to have to lay off employees. Instead, we hired new workers to keep pace with the growth.)

WHEN RELATIONSHIPS NEED HELP

In a best-case scenario, your relationship with your employees is healthy and robust. Of course, in Europe, we also have unions, due to several factors like the decrease of blue-collar jobs (replaced by technicians and white collars), digitization (leading to more autonomous jobs), and globalization (enhancing the international competition on labor costs). In Italy, they mostly represent retired workers. In Germany, they work in accordance with the employers, having also the right to appoint workers to the Board of Directors. In France, they are still quite strong, representing especially the public sector workers.

One can debate how unions help or hinder a business; however, it is strange to watch how in America the very people who have traditionally been helped by unions have been turned against them. In general, when I consider how the relations between American business owners, employees, consumers, and the general public have evolved, I see a wasted opportunity to strengthen and fortify a business against coming challenges.

Over the past few centuries, there has been a general trend that employees can work fewer hours and still earn enough to support themselves and their families. In the mid-nineteenth century, housemaids and other servants in England and the US worked fourteen-to-seventeen-hour days with only half of Sunday off. In 1908, a New England mill was the first company to grant workers two days of rest per week, as opposed to the more usual model of half of Saturday of rest and Sunday for worship. This new idea of a five-day workweek was embraced during the Great Depression in the hopes that shorter hours would help curb unemployment.[3] Every sign pointed forward to a future where workers would work less: in 1928, economist John Maynard Keynes predicted that technological improvements would reduce the workweek to fifteen hours by 2028.

This, obviously, did not happen. Instead, the gradual shift toward shorter hours has reversed for management-level employees, who often find themselves working essentially all the time. Hourly workers, such as those in England with the rise of "zero-hour contracts," have the opposite problem, struggling to get enough hours on a consistent basis to cover their costs and pay their bills. Neither of these options is conducive to happy relations between employer and employees. More important, they are counterproductive, creating stress and resentment among the people who are the backbone of your business.

Today we *all* live in a volatile world. There is little certainty about the future. Our English friends are embarking on life outside of the EU. America is entering into life after Trump.

We need to consider things as varied as climate change, global competition, wealth inequality, and political instability as we plan for the coming decades. In your business you might have different concerns. Perhaps the political instability that is currently percolating across the globe threatens your markets, or you are feeling the pressure to cut costs. The instinct is always to chip away at the benefits, wages, or hours of your employees. However, this can backfire, especially if these cuts aren't universal.

Why not try making life *better* instead of worse for your workers? In America, the CEO of a card-processing company called Gravity Payments took a 90 percent pay cut in order to pay all his employees a minimum $70,000 salary. This was both lauded and controversial. Twenty people suddenly had their pay increase by a third or so. They were delighted! However, some higher-paid employees were angry to find that their entry-level coworkers were suddenly earning the same as them. The owner's brother sued him, and some suggested his move was more self-serving than altruistic. Yet the business is currently growing, with double the employees it had at the time of the increase. Perhaps most interesting, their employees are feeling more confident to take on long-term financial responsibilities and commitments by starting families in far greater numbers than they were before the wage increase.

Other companies are freeing white-collar workers from the stress of commuting by allowing them to set their own hours and telecommute. This trend has grown exponentially during the pandemic. We found that our company operated just as well with employees at home as it did when they were in the office. Of course, these kinds of benefits mean nothing to manual laborers who have to report for duty come what may.

Perhaps this is too extreme, but at its core, the idea of creating a more equitable business model can actually help you build your company. You might not have a family-run business, but by treating your employees as more than weak ties, you can begin to build a relationship with them that is durable enough to resist the problems of the future.

Imagine how this Italian idea of relationships might work in your own business. What would you have to do to make working for you so rewarding that your employees are literally handing their jobs on to their children? It isn't simply financial; we offer good wages, but not dramatically more than our competitors. Nor is it always about extra perks or privileges. Instead it is a bigger overarching ethos that we practice every day: we are all in this together.

What aspect of your business is truly unifying? For us, illy is an almost organic institution. It lives and breathes with a shared history that is passed from generation to generation. We share a pride in what we do. Where is the pride in your organization? Do you understand what your employees tell their friends and new acquaintances about their work? If you don't know, ask them to explain to you what your business is and what it means. Ask them to tell you the moments they've experienced that make them proud to be identified with your business.

These moments that transcend employment or obligation, that are about something more elemental and emotional, will give you clues about how you can improve the experience of working in your organization, even if you are not able to unilaterally raise wages or improve benefits. Perhaps you own some kind of transportation company. You may believe you are in the business of getting people from A to B, but your drivers or attendants see things differently. What brings them joy, what makes them feel connected to your company, are those brief moments when they realize they have reunited a family, gotten a jobseeker to an important interview, or otherwise been part of an emotional and deeply personal moment. If you can recognize this, then there is a way to strengthen your bond with your employee, to give them one more reason to take that bit of pride in their job. And, of course, once you are able to act on this realization, it will only improve your customers' experience of using your services.

TEN

PATIENCE

wasn't a patient person before being elected mayor of Trieste in 1993; I always looked for quick answers, changes, and results. Maybe this was because my grandfather Riccardo died as a civilian during World War II at the age of forty. I had an anxious feeling that I would follow the same destiny: dying young before I had accomplished what I set out to do in life. This feeling compelled me to rush through my life, accomplishing as much as I could in the business at an early age.

When, to my relief, I did not die young, I realized I might have more time than I had imagined. I was able to expand my focus, and I ran for public office, seeking to improve the well-being of my city, Trieste.

LEARNING PATIENCE

A local government is like a conglomerate of companies delivering many different services, with tangled layers of governance in a layered and intertwined legal environment. (Perhaps that is why I feel at home running a complicated organization like Polo del Gusto!) Italians especially love our regulations and bureaucracy: during my time as mayor, it sometimes felt like everyone from the stray cats in the piazza on up needed to share their opinion on any decision.

Frustrating, yes, but it was a good education in collaboration in a complex work environment. After all, if you don't learn to manage this complexity, you won't deliver results. It took eight years of my two terms as a mayor and seven more years of my successor's to complete the highway connection leading out of the city. My days were spent meeting people and understanding their often-conflicting needs. Sometimes I had to talk to people whose lives were going to be upended by choices I had to make, such as changing local laws that would adversely affect their businesses. They were going to be unhappy with my choices, and I truly felt their pain. I had to learn to feel empathy for the struggling people of my town.

In the mayor's office, I finally earned something that had always evaded me: patience. It takes a long time to make good things happen, either in a municipality or an organization. You will be tempted to change course on your way to that good destination. And at times you will feel compelled to make drastic changes when you do not immediately succeed. Yet, every time I succeeded it was because of a kind of vertical and horizontal coherence. I continued in the same direction: toward that highway, or that new municipal ruling, or that new infrastructure investment. It took empathy, it took conviction, but most of all it took patience.

When I say, "Have patience," I am encouraging you to hold on to the things that make your business work. I am also suggesting that the kind of change that revitalizes a struggling company or town can take time. You will be pressured to make the wrong kind of change, slashing your most experienced (and expensive) employees or downgrading your raw materials to lower-quality goods. However, if you are making a truly great product, one that is superior quality, that has surprised and delighted your customer, you will always have a market for what you do. Eventually, when the economy is restored or society feels more stable, your customers will return in their former numbers. However, if you have diluted your product, substituting inferior ingredients, or lowering production standards, they will not stay for long. Instead, they will lose trust in you and depart for good. So, have faith, hold on to the authentic core of your business, but continue to refine the elements that aren't working.

There are two types of patience in business: constructive patience, when you are building something new; and ongoing patience, when you need to maintain an existing enterprise. Finally, there is the problematic side of patience: stagnation, where indecision and doubt leads to prolonged inaction. Knowing the difference between these three states, and how to respond to each of them, is key.

DOMORI: CONSTRUCTIVE PATIENCE

I have experienced the delicate balancing act of nurturing a new company from the red to the black many times in my life. As an Incanto business, everything that illy does prioritizes long-term sustainability over short-term profits, and quality over a short-lived bounce in sales. This is easy to accept when times are good, harder during tough times such as when a recession looms. As with my mayoral life, I nurtured coherence, constantly asking myself if my choices and decisions were keeping our businesses on the same specific path. Most recently, I experienced this constructive patience with Domori, as I nurtured them through a difficult post-acquisition phase.

Gruppo illy bought Domori in 2007. Like illy, they are a short-recipe company. And again like illy, they prioritize exceptional raw materials, a unique supply chain, and sustainability—a blessing to the people who grow the raw materials. All of these reasons made me see that there was a deeper value to Domori than simply its immediate potential. Like illy, Domori had a unique strategy, pursuing refined, surprising, Incanto quality, even when most chocolatiers were falling back on overroasted beans, artificial flavors, novelties like chocolate with hot peppers, and low-grade, easily sourced cacao.

I was convinced of the potential of the company. Even more so, I was convinced that Domori was uniquely valuable to illy Group because its vision was aligned with ours. Another conglomerate wouldn't have recognized that value. Indeed, it might have seen that insistence on quality as a burden rather than a blessing.

I knew that even though sales were only about a couple of million euros, Domori was a smart purchase. I also knew that some time was needed to reach profitability through growth. We would have to spend money, first by hiring a managing director and at least three functional managers to take care of the production, sales, and administration. We also made many important investments, like the brand-new production line for professional chocolate that cost about two million euros. After some years of growth but also losses, and with the need of repeated capital injections, some of the board members became impatient, asking me to solve the problem quickly. Instead I persisted, tending to Domori like a young tree or vine, and looking to the future when it would deliver fruit. It took twelve years and twenty million euros in sales to finally break even, yet, by the time it did, Domori was a resilient and strong branch of the Polo del Gusto tree. This is because we had patience with it; we allowed the company to grow on its own terms without slashing payroll, cutting costs, or selling it when the profits were slow to come.

Our investment paid off during 2020 and the COVID-19 pandemic. Not only did Domori repeat its previous year's sales figures, but it also continued to expand both within and outside of Italy, with improving good financial results. It took a lot of patience to let the "baby" grow, especially when I had to listen to people who felt less confident of the company's long-term prospects. I had faith, however. The feelings I had were the same as when I had started at illy in 1977. I saw a company with a big potential, still unexploited. But illy at that time was already forty-four years old. When I had those same feelings about Domori in 2007, it was only ten years old. It needed more time to grow, mature, and become "adult."

I could have quickly brought Domori's financial statements to a balance, just by cutting some costs. We could have let go of some of those managers or diluted the chocolate with a few extra ingredients. These changes would have brought us into the black in a short time. However, these changes would have irreparably broken the trust that Domori customers had in the brand. And it would have prevented the company from becoming an important player in the high-quality chocolate industry. To get to this position, it needed to grow, and to grow we needed to patiently inject more money.

ILLY COFFEE: ONGOING PATIENCE

With people, as with anything else, the output depends on the input. You will get in proportion to what you give. If the input consists not only of professional skills but also of humanity, kindness, friendship, and empathy, then the output will be a full involvement in the spirit of the company. People not only have arms and brains; they also have hearts. If the company culture is involved and shared, the workplace is pleasant, and the managers involve the workers' brains and hearts, their work will also include giving ideas, suggesting innovations and improvements, and doing their job better than required. This is particularly important for companies producing top-quality goods, the Incanto companies, where the human touch to get the best quality makes the difference.

You can see this in action on the illy factory floor. First thing in the morning all our employees, from the CEO on down to the newest blue-collar worker, gather around the coffee bar. Our suppliers and customers, visiting the factory, are also squeezed in. It's a moment for relaxing, taking a breath, and socializing. "Coffee time" is 9:00 a.m., but our employees can come to the coffee bar at any time; it's a kind of rite. The coffee is free; conversation is encouraged. A prospective client from Germany might laugh at a roughly translated joke told by an old-timer who has worked her whole life on the shop floor. At the very least, he walks away with a sense that this is a functional and happy company. (These days, of course, we are more careful, allowing only a few people at a time to congregate. I look forward to the moment when we can fully return to this old habit, and CEOs, blue collars, clients, and suppliers can once more meet as friends and equals around a caffe.)

Later in the day, our workers will meet again in the cafeteria for lunch, for a meal of locally sourced food, prepared fresh every morning. illy subsidizes the cost, making sure that a good and nourishing meal is available and affordable to all. The atmosphere in the cafeteria is familiar and friendly. Blue and white collars, managers and shareholders all eat in the same area, often talking from one table to the other. Later, at dinner, the managers and white collars go home, leaving the evening shift to a rowdier and louder conversation over a dinner of spaghetti or penne.

Throughout the year we organize small celebrations. St. Nicholas, Christmas, and Easter feasts are organized for the children of the workers. They laugh in delight, hunting for presents or chattering over full plates of food. Finally, in July, before closing for vacation in August, a big feast including food, drinks, and music is organized by a team of workers. All our employees bring their families and share in a final feast before the office closes. This is as much about solidarity as it is about entertaining our workers. If we are an extended family, then we must celebrate as one.

I think this solidarity is less about compensation than it is about culture, and this gives you an opportunity. The world is full of businesses that might pay a little more but will drain the life out of the people who work for them. If you can offer something better, perhaps a job that will not sap your workers of their joy and passion for life, then you have a meaningful proposition to make to them. In the last chapter we mentioned Gravity. They based their $70,000 salary floor on studies that have shown that one's happiness plateaus once one earns $75,000 a year. At this level of income people know they can meet their basic needs in life. They will not go hungry, and their kids will be warm and well cared for (this is not necessarily true for cities such as New York or London, but otherwise is generally accurate).

To keep the most skilled people, a company needs first of all a good culture that includes a commitment to all the stakeholders. First, to the employees, which means paying them better than the market, training them, and offering a pleasant place of work.

Above all, the management of the company should transmit to the workers the feeling of participating in a great project, so as to involve their pride. When more generations of workers of the same family are employed in the same company and a positive company climate is nourished day by day, the risk of losing the most skilled workers is minimized.

This kind of patience is the same belief that a farmer brings to his fields, or a vintner brings to her grapes: I must tend to the people I rely on, ensuring that working for me is a sustainable, joyful endeavor. This takes patience and constant, minute adjustments to the flow of work and the culture within our companies. It's not easy. I offer a carrot, not a stick, even though sticks sometimes get superficially faster results.

I always remember a friend who worked at an independent advertising agency in Florida. The new owner organized a summer party and invited every employee, plus one guest, promising it would be an annual event. The next year, however, the owner traded his carrot for a stick, and organized an overnight two-day party, to which only the "best" employees were invited. He thought he was motivating his employees to work harder and be recognized. Instead, the bulk of his employees were now angry, embarrassed, and hurt. The agency floundered, shedding employees before eventually being absorbed into a global agency and disappearing forever.

AUTOMATION AND FACING THE FUTURE

We of course have had to balance our care for our employees with the reality of increasing automation. This will be the big dilemma of business in the twenty-first century, and it is something I consider often. However, unlike many of my contemporaries, I am hopeful about a future where automation and happy, well-cared-for employees are not mutually exclusive.

Some industries have been decimated by changes in technology. I worry about the demise of local retail as consumers turn more and more to online shopping. Italy has traditionally been resilient to innovations in online shopping. We prefer to shop in person and ideally use cash. The small-to-medium-sized, family-run businesses of Italy employ 78 percent of our workforce. We have regulations that protect independent businesses (such as pharmacies) over chains[1] though some argue this stymies innovation. Our rough rural roads and patchy broadband are another impediment to widespread reliance on the internet. However, with the coronavirus, that changed. In 2019, 40 percent of Italians shopped online (compared to 87 percent in Britain and 79 percent in Germany).[2] During the pandemic, this number almost doubled. Amazon, the largest of these online portals, is opening new fulfillment centers across Italy while facing angry unions striking over poor sanitation and health-care measures.[3] At the same time, many people want more fulfillment centers and the employment they bring (even as they threaten the jobs of people already working at existing companies).

I have hope that after the initial disruption settles, Italy will find a balance between the convenience of online shopping and the small businesses and shops that are at the heart of our local communities. It has happened before. When steam engines were invented, and trains substituted horse coaches (with a much higher efficiency), the coach drivers said that the unemployment rate would rise sharply. This didn't happen and won't happen today.

Progress produces new jobs (before automatizing, some-one must build the automatic machines and then someone else will maintain them), increasing productivity and wages (allowing workers to purchase additional or better goods), and stimulating an overall improvement of the goods/services produced (something that generally requires more labor). Since I started working at illy in 1977, we have increased the quantities of coffee produced twenty times and the number of employees about ten times. We have never laid off anyone. We have only hired new people (with increasing levels of education, thus better paid). Improving the quality is the best way to increase efficiency without increasing the unemployment rate.

These days, many of the operations on the illy factory floor have been automated. The atmosphere in the illy factory is "relaxedly busy"; the production is totally automated and all the machines work rhythmically to fill, condition, seal, and package the different-sized containers. At the end of the production lines, robots palletize the cases and finally wrap them in a film. illy employees dressed in smocks and caps branded with "illy" walk calmly among the machines, watching that everything flows properly and intervening only if needed to unlock a machine or to fill its reservoir.

As we move forward in business and culture, a focus on superior manufacturing and raw materials will be our best defense against automation and the end of employment. At illy, our employees are primarily focused on ensuring quality. They monitor machines to make sure they are roasting at the right temperature and grinding to the correct dimension. They double-check packaging to confirm it is flawless and that no one will be buying a dented tin of coffee. The more rigorously we insist on quality, the more we will rely on our employees, who allow us to prioritize it.

PATIENCE, NOT STAGNATION

If I could change one thing about how my American contemporaries respond to downturns in their business, or other setbacks, it would be this: understand and embrace the idea of holding on to your good employees and all their hard-earned skill and valuable institutional knowledge for as long as possible. Understand and accept your role in the larger ecosystem of your community. I will never understand how companies run by some of the most entrepreneurial and ambitious people in the world can jettison employees as an instinctive response to a difficult moment in their business. Or worse: build business models that are explicitly designed to convert previously reliable full-time jobs into seasonal or part-time work. Nothing good comes out of creating resentment and anger between management and employees, especially when job insecurity or disappearing benefits are dressed up as freedom or choice as in the case of many app-based delivery and ride-share businesses.

True, we are not perfect in Italy. Many of our large private and state-run enterprises are floundering due to patience's opposing twin: stagnation. None more so than our flagship airline, Alitalia, which after eleven years of being poorly managed by private groups, and three attempts at restructuring (all unsuccessful), was taken over by the government in 2020. Mired in dysfunction, employee squabbles, and debt, these are not good places to work. (Alitalia is jokingly said to stand for "Always Late in Takeoff, Always Late in Arrival"). This causes great distress within our borders. After all, Alitalia *is* Italy. Anita Ekberg flies into Rome on a DC-6B in *La Dolce Vita*. The green-and-red livery, with its "A" tail insignia, was once as common in Cairo, New York, Sao Paulo, and Tokyo as it was in Milan or Rome. Both left-wing and right-wing governments have thrown hundreds of millions of euros at the airline to keep it aloft. Still, as one financier noted, investing more money in Alitalia is like pouring water through a spaghetti strainer.[4] Patience is one thing, but patience must also be engaged, thoughtful, and considered.

In Alitalia's case, we have hurt ourselves by refusing to adapt when change is inevitable. Most Italians now travel on budget carriers such as EasyJet, which though originally British, now flies out of bases all over Europe as various EasyJet subsidiaries (it remains to be seen how Brexit may affect this). Alitalia's new management would do well to show patience with their staff and think creatively about how to transition into the modern era a business that directly employs 11,000 people and countless other third-party workers. As of now, no one is fully willing to commit to restructuring the airline in a way that makes sense in the modern world. It makes no sense to protect a national flagship airline. Instead, what we need is a European airline that can compete with the American, Middle East, and Chinese carriers. For now, Alitalia, along with other flagship carriers like Air France and Lufthansa, remains a "zombie airline," sucking up vast amounts of taxpayer money and potentially running afoul of EU rules on state aid.[5]

Still, for the most part, Italian family-run businesses understand that we are nothing without the deep institutional knowledge of our best employees. Indeed, with our tradition of keeping jobs within the same family for generations, this knowledge becomes more deeply ingrained in the people who work for us.

There is, of course, a cost to prioritizing your employees' well-being, and we have touched on it throughout the book. You will spend more to create an environment that is pleasant to work in. You will lose days or weeks of work with generous vacation arrangements. But be patient: any investment in the well-being of your employees will pay dividends. I think of my relationships with my employees the same way I think of those thousand-year-old olive trees or vines that must be pruned and nurtured for years before their first harvest. If I take time to tend to their well-being, they will repay me with decades of good work.

FAZIOLI

The Illys are a musical family. My grandmother played every day, as do many of my cousins. My father educated me to love classical music (as I write, I'm listening to Mahler's Symphony no. 4). As mayor of Trieste, I was also the chairman of the Teatro Lirico Giuseppe Verdi (founded in 1801). There, one evening, I listened to a concerto played on a Fazioli piano, manufactured a few miles away, between Trieste and Venice. The *bel canto*[6] resonance of the piano was sublime, both agile and silky, skipping lightly over the notes, but with astonishing power and depth of tone. Later, I learned that Fazioli ambassadors prize the pianos for the way they maintain a rich timbre on all musical textures, even at very low sound levels. Upon further inquiry, I realized that the Fazioli piano company was then only thirty years old and positioning itself as a bold upstart in the staid and conventional world of piano builders.

It takes three months to make a Ferrari. Even so, the Ferrari factory in Maranello manages to make 8,400 cars a year. One cashmere goat produces only four ounces of undercoat (the part of its coat that is spun into yarn) in a year. However, there are enough cashmere-producing goats in the world that you never have to wait to buy a sweater. Twelve thousand of the famed Hermès Birkin bags are produced every year. Still, with the right phone number and enough money, you will never have to wait long to buy one.

Fazioli, unlike Ferrari or Hermès, produces no more than 140 products a year. If you want a Fazioli grand piano, you must be prepared to wait. Of course, pianos, by their nature, require patience. It takes decades to master the instrument, and almost as long to discard one if you grow tired of it (if only because of the great difficulty of removing one from a house: windows and even walls must be taken down first). If it is moved carelessly, it may dig ruts into a parquet ballroom floor that will never come out. It requires the care and attention of a tuner on a regular basis. However, a truly great piano, such as a Fazioli, repays your devotion with sounds so rich and resonant they illuminate and enliven every note, be they played pianissimo or fortissimo.

I soon arranged a visit to the factory, in my role of president of Friuli Venezia Giulia. The founder, Paolo Fazioli, met me and showed me around the calm and serene factory floor. The factory wasn't as large as I expected. However, it was well organized, everything in its place and perfectly cleaned. The workers, dressed in matching green coats, worked with calm and precision. Occasionally one would play a note to test the setting of a string or the strike of a hammer, listening to it with his head cocked to one side and an expression of utter focus and concentration on his face. Then he would gently adjust the mechanism of the piano by a fraction of a millimeter, until the sound was perfect. I immediately understood that each movement was critical. To prevent an irreparable flaw, Fazioli[7] inspects each component of every piano at every step during the construction. Given the small number of pianos and the high cost of each, it would be problematic to have to reject a piano and deem it unfit for sale.

Paolo Fazioli confirmed this, telling me, "Accuracy in the work is essential! I have had the opportunity to visit many piano factories. I have always noticed very high production rates! Our aim is uncompromising quality."

Fazioli is famous for making the biggest grand piano, ten feet long. More than that, though, they are renowned for the bold and audacious style they bring to their designs: an art deco–inspired swoosh that looks more like a stylized yacht than a musical instrument, or an organic design that suggests the roots of a tree growing up from the floor to embrace the pianist. Fazioli will work with a customer to bring their vision to life, though, as he says, he sometimes needs to lead a client toward better aesthetic choices. The wood comes from the forest of Tarvisio (in the mountainous region). The high elevation and low temperatures mean that the trees grow very slowly, producing a harmonic wood that is then aged to become even more select.

I asked Paolo what inspired the astonishing visual designs of his pianos: "Being Italian—of the most beautiful country in the world—makes us very proud," he told me, "especially for me who was born in Rome and did all my studies there. Living close to these churches, squares, fountains, palaces, monuments, vestiges of the Roman era has enriched and enriches us, leading us to beauty.

"When I started building my pianos, it was natural to revise the design and proportions of the piano while respecting tradition, making its image 'Italian.'"

More astonishing yet is the length of time it takes to build the pianos: two years. Paolo Fazioli is an engineer by trade, albeit one who loves music. He combined those two passions to develop a new system for building pianos, with the objective of getting the optimal sound. The different steps of the production process each need a long time. In between each step, the pianos must rest and age further as well. At the end of two years, the sound of the piano is full, elegant, clean, round, and smooth. A sound you can recognize among tens of other pianos' sounds.

What I learn from Fazioli is that patience is easy when you have conviction and a vision. When you know 100 percent what you want to do, and how you wish to do it (build the greatest piano with great care and sparing no expense), then you are willing to keep going throughout even the most testing scenario. This is just as true if your business is something simpler. I have had many friends over the years who built businesses based on their particular dream. Often, they struggle, desperately trying to pay their bills or to simply keep the business afloat from one month to the next.

The ones who truly believe in what they are doing, who see a vision even decades away, are the ones who succeed and keep going, even when the world laughs at them. They are diligent in seeking accuracy and quality in all things. They hold true to a vision of success that others might not yet see. One of my friends struggled to get a creative business off the ground. Years later he acknowledged that he'd been so poor he'd taken the city bus to important meetings rather than drive a car of his own, as any successful entrepreneur would be expected to. Yet his confidence and clarity about where he was going, and why, paid off. Today he is a powerful player in his field.

Yes, it is important to adjust and evolve what you are doing as you experience small failures and successes. It may be necessary to change the way you move toward your vision, perhaps working for a larger company rather than progressing as an independent. However, never be embarrassed that your ambitions haven't come to fruition just yet. Never be despondent that your work is not seen or acknowledged right now.

With patience, conviction, and vision, you will succeed. Hold on to your vision, let others judge if they must, but be certain about what you are doing, and why.

As Paolo says, "Our pianos are certainly different, I am not the one who should say if they are better or worse than others. But diversity contributes to beauty, and in the world we live in, beauty is what we all need."

And, equally important, never write yourself off as "too old" or having had a big idea or vision too late in your life to try. As much as I love music, I have never become adept at an instrument. Now, at a later stage in life, I think I would like to learn to play piano and finally join in with my relatives and their love of playing. It's never too late to open a new door and walk through.

ELEVEN

SURPRISE

A number of years ago, I traveled to Cologne to meet with Adolfo Massi, owner of Mastrojanni's German distributor. Massi, a consummate gentleman, invited me to a memorable dinner one evening. Excellent cuisine, fascinating guests, sparkling conversation. Most astonishing, however, was the immense wooden table on which the meal was served.

The first surprise was the table's sheer size: over twenty-five feet in length. The second was its peculiar shape. While the top was a plane, the sides were all jagged edges and sinuous swoops. The third, its texture. Marveling, I put my hand to the table's flat surface, expecting perhaps the smoothness of laminate or the glossy tackiness of shellac varnish. Instead, the tips of my fingers encountered an unexpected silkiness—a finish achieved, I later learned, with a recipe containing only natural substances like beeswax. I have never felt anything quite like it.

As we sat down to eat, Massi delivered the fourth and largest surprise of the night. He explained that this gargantuan piece of furniture had been made entirely by hand from a single log of Kauri wood, famous for its shimmering, golden luster. Since living Kauri trees are protected in New Zealand, the wood for this table had been dredged from the bottom of a prehistoric swamp. Tens of thousands of years ago, tsunamis swept many of these mighty trees down. Preserved by the swamp for millennia, ancient Kauri is the world's oldest workable wood. Extracting a three-hundred-ton tree trunk from the mud isn't easy, even with excavators and bulldozers, but the quality is unparalleled, and the living trees are preserved. This is the ultimate form of recycling.

Massi's table was surprising. I had never seen anything quite like it; sheer delight held my attention. There was much to appreciate about it: The sides were sealed with an all-natural clear resin, otherwise left just as the wood had emerged from the swamp. The same resin filled any holes in the surface of the table to ensure perfect smoothness and uniformity. Despite this reliance on natural ingredients, or perhaps because of it, the table is dramatically resilient in the face of the elements. Massi had left it out in the sun and rain for extended periods with no damage whatsoever.

Later, Massi told me that he owned *another* such table, this one forty feet in length and weighing more than four tons. It was sitting in his warehouse awaiting a suitable space.

What kind of company would go to such lengths to build a dining table? We were in Germany, but I felt right away that the table must be Italian, and I was right: Riva 1920 is based in Cantù, a city in the northern Lombardy region. Later, curious to see more, I visited their factory hoping to learn more about how the greatest Italian companies employ the element of surprise to delight their customers.

THE ELEMENTS OF SURPRISE

A handful of companies astonish as a matter of habit. Surprise is an integral part of their culture. Steve Jobs's "one more thing" was the most anticipated part of his annual presentation. Apple under Jobs simply wasn't finished making something until a unique, unexpected flourish had been incorporated into every aspect of the product, from its core function to its packaging. Companies like Apple continually seek to elevate the customer experience beyond the status quo. Meeting expectations would never suffice.

Italian businesses are exceptionally passionate about their products. They settle for nothing less than customer delight. Italian businesses abhor mediocrity. From our perspective, it's better to attempt something unexpected and risk appearing foolish than settle for adequate. This is true even in the most innocuous industries. Blame our history. Art is Italy's lifeblood. Our businesses bring playfulness and creative inspiration to everything we produce.

So, how does surprise actually work on the level of a product's conception and design? How do the best companies consistently pull it off? I have found that it comes down to knowledge: you must understand consumer expectations in order to upset them. No product is entirely new in terms of its function. As revolutionary as it was, the first automobile was still referred to as a "horseless carriage." In fact, we continue to measure engines in terms of horsepower today.

Similarly, a groundbreaking product like the first iPod was initially judged in comparison with portable music players available at the time. Those early MP3 players seemed astonishing. You could carry five hundred songs with you wherever you went! Now, of course, that capacity seems archaic compared to streaming and unlimited music. The iPod surprised consumers because it offered an elegant, intuitive interface in contrast to the clunky, arcane MP3 players. Those original iPods with their black-and-white screens and circular interfaces are now like the MP3 players that came before them, shoved to the back of drawers, forgotten. They have been replaced by the "all-in-one" experience of the iPhone. And this is an important truth about the quality of surprise: it works best by starting with what customers understand and taking it in an unexpected direction.

The existing products in a category establish a set of customer expectations. Operating as though these expectations don't exist leads to failure; this is the line between surprise and bafflement. True surprise is designed through a genuine understanding of what those expectations are. Riva 1920 astonishes with its furniture because it takes all of our accepted notions about what furniture is, how it's made, and what it looks and feels like—and subverts them.

We all love surprises. Surprise may seem abstract or intangible, but that doesn't mean it isn't crucial to the survival of any business in a competitive market. The economist Theodore Levitt, then a professor at Harvard Business School, wrote that there is always a crucial, intangible element to any product or service. As he put it, that, "'something' . . . helps determine from whom they'll buy, what they'll pay, and whether, in the view of the seller, they're 'loyal' or 'fickle.'"[1]

This is the heart of offering a product of Incanto, and the idea of augmented quality, simply, a way to give your customer more than they were expecting: to surprise, delight, and enchant them. This distinction between expected and augmented is the quality that produces surprise, the "wow" effect. Intangible, yes, but necessary.

Of course, doing something unexpected that surprises your customers is a risk. They may not like it. Your product's touch of individuality might not appeal to them, might even actively turn off some prospective customers. Yet, it is in this unexpected place, between what is expected and what is unknown, that you have the greatest chance to create a connection with your customers. It happens on a physical level. When we are surprised, a little burst of dopamine in the brain delights us. If surprise makes customers happy and all it requires is an understanding of expectations and a willingness to play with them, why don't all companies build surprising products? The simple answer is fear. Fear isn't a problem for Maurizio Riva, president of Riva 1920. Italy, he says, is a country "that does not give in."

COURAGEOUS CREATION

Riva 1920 believes in the value of a singular vision over design by committee. It contracts with artists and creatives like the Albanian sculptor Helidon Xhixha and the Italian architect Marco Piva to shape an initial piece in marble, steel, wood, or a combination of materials. Then, as explained by Maurizio Riva, they will "see how it goes, if and how many we sell."

It takes a good deal of conviction to trust any product's design to one person, no matter how well established they may be as an artist or designer. Risk and surprise go hand in hand.

A FAILURE TO SURPRISE

Today, most mass-market products aim solely to meet market expectations at a competitive price. Yet, how tragic to miss an opportunity to surprise or delight your customers. I see too many organizations that funnel all of their creativity into advertising, perhaps surprising us with a celebrity spokesperson, or joke, or unexpected "twist." Why? These superficial surprises in a commercial, or on a billboard, work on a level where they create a mental link between the customer and the brand, but they don't offer anything more substantive to keep reinforcing that connection. We've all seen airplane or tourism campaigns that suggest your travel to a distant land will be delightful and full of unexpected experiences. Yet, when the time comes to board the flight or check into the hotel, we realize there is nothing there but the same dispiriting, dirty aircraft and overcrowded beach. The purpose of surprise is to so delight your customer that they will always be curious and interested to return to your product, anticipating either the same experience of augmented quality or a new one.

Companies that fail to surprise don't do so by accident. There is safety in numbers. If a group of industry veterans makes all of its product decisions to meet widely accepted industry norms, who can find fault with them, even if the product fails? There might have been a more interesting, more delightful way, but you can't fault someone for doing things as they've always been done, meeting the bar instead of raising it.

Adult customers often let boring companies get away with their stubborn lack of imagination. We are tired, overworked, distracted. But our children are less forgiving. They demand surprise in return for their precious allowance money, even in lieu of quality. Nearly every successful children's product incorporates the unexpected. In Europe, our children plead for Kinder Joy eggs; they know that each chocolate shell contains a small toy. It is impossible to guess what it might be from the outside of the foil-wrapped candy, and this unexpectedness only makes them more eager to crack it open.

In the United States, Cracker Jack, the sugar-coated popcorn and peanut snack considered the very first junk food, promised a "Toy Surprise" in each box. The novelty item might have been a ring, a plastic figure, or something else equally small and trivial. But it wasn't the quality of the trinkets that made Cracker Jack an essential purchase at baseball games for over a century. It was the element of surprise. The brand's current owner, Frito-Lay, dispensed with physical items in 2016, but a QR code in each box leads to a mobile game. To this day, a box containing only Cracker Jacks remains unthinkable. As a snack, they aren't very good, but as an experience, they are delightful.

Adults are harder to surprise and, as a result, we learn to go without it most of the time, prioritizing function and price over delight. This presupposes a trade-off, as though surprise is an additional cost that must be offset. In reality, surprise requires only creativity and courage. This is the opening that breakthrough products exploit. They remain competitive in terms of price and features and go above and beyond to surprise customers as well. It's an unbeatable formula and one that all great Italian businesses follow.

My wife, Rossana, is a sommelier and an instructor of sommeliers. She samples the world's finest vintages on a regular basis and, as you can imagine, possesses an extraordinarily refined palate. All her life, she had avoided chocolate, finding nothing interesting in it. Then, a few years ago, she sampled a Criollo dark chocolate by Domori. In that moment, everything changed. Rossana's expectations about chocolate were completely upset. She knew what chocolate was supposed to taste like but, while Domori met that expectation by tasting like chocolate, it vastly exceeded her expectations of chocolate's complexity and quality. The degree of augmentation was such that, when Rossana went on a health retreat with dietary restrictions, it was chocolate, not wine, that she missed the most.

Though a failure to surprise may feel safer to an organization, over the long term, it is actually incredibly risky. Yes, the market will tolerate an adequate product *if* it's the only option at that price. Such an offering is vulnerable, however. If a competitor matches it in price and quality and adds an element of surprise, the child in these adult customers awakens and they switch in droves.

Many well-established makers of quality products have failed because they weren't willing to surprise customers until they themselves were taken by surprise by a bolder competitor. Simply meeting market expectations is not sufficient to defend your position in a category. To sustain unmatchable excellence, you must risk surprise or risk losing everything.

ENGINEERING CUSTOMER DELIGHT

Riva 1920 produces a limited number of its signature tables each year. Each one is unique, simply because the rare and difficult-to-source materials make uniformity impossible. Of course, any kind of handmade creation is naturally going to be distinctive. If anything, it's harder to achieve uniformity by hand.

It is only through personalized goods that you can truly meet the unique expectations of each and every buyer.[2] The Kauri tables by Riva 1920 do this at great cost and effort, but as technological developments like 3D printing, artificial intelligence, and robotization continue to progress, it will become more and more feasible for all companies to respond to their own segments of one.

On the other hand, mass-produced items can offer unique elements, too—a special-order paint job on an Alfa Romeo, for example. Physical variety isn't the only way to subvert a customer's expectations either. The customer's experience of the product can be unique even if the product itself is mass-produced. Riva 1920 does this on multiple levels: a Riva table isn't the typical size. It takes your mind a moment to adjust to the unexpected scale. Many high-tech products achieve a similar surprise through miniaturization and packing ever more features into smaller and lighter gadgets. Riva goes in the other direction. Instead of being sized to fit proportionally within the typical dining area, Riva's creations demand that the would-be owner move other things, even tearing out walls to make room.

The tables have an unusual shape, the sides left raw to create a startling effect. My first thought was that I might get a splinter sitting along that edge. Yet when I touched it, I realized that lustrous resin meant it actually felt smooth. Nothing about its silky texture matches your expectations either. These aesthetic surprises, one after the other, are captivating. A Riva 1920 table is *mozzafiato*: breathtaking.

Riva's ability to surprise and delight is built into every facet of its furniture, from the ancient wood dredged from swamps to the secret, all-natural recipes used. No solvents or artificial chemicals play any role in the manufacturing. The owners of a Riva 1920 piece take pride in having discovered the company and acquiring one of its products. Almost inevitably they share the story of the table with their friends and acquaintances. This word-of-mouth is crucial. Riva 1920 has struggled with the dealers who sell its furniture around the world. Many haven't been naturally skilled at telling its story. To rectify this, dealers are invited to visit the factory in Cantù.

These visitors stay at a nearby farm and spend several days immersed in the company's culture and philosophy. If they can't come to Italy, Maurizio will visit them personally. This kind of education is key to any business that is aiming to surprise its customers.

When you are offering augmented quality, there will inevitably be some explaining to do: just as our customers must be educated to appreciate the nuances of our product, so may yours. While this approach is a bit more expensive than printing a color brochure, it is essential to achieving the intended surprise: the story must be told properly for customers to fully appreciate the delightfulness of each piece.

THE FOUNDATIONS OF SURPRISE

Riva 1920 is a family business with a strong sense of tradition. Maurizio Riva's grandfather started the company at the age of twenty-eight. Later, Maruizio took it over, becoming the third generation to lead the company. It would have been completely expected for him to trim the fat, at least in the places most customers wouldn't notice. A few bold, cost-cutting measures would have signaled Maurizio's willingness to break with the old and boost profits for him, his brother, and their families. In fact, to your average CEO, the company's methods must look as in need of a trim as the unfinished sides of a Riva table do to your average carpenter.

However, Maurizio is not your average CEO. At least he's not typical of the CEOs you see outside of Italy. Under his leadership, the company has held tight to its traditions. Riva 1920 continues to rely on solid wood in all its creations. This wood is either reforested, meaning it was replaced by new plants, or reclaimed in creative ways, from the ancient Kauri already discussed to the use of *bricole*. Tens of thousands of these oak pylons mark navigable channels in the canals and lagoons of Venice. When the wood of an individual *bricola* begins to deteriorate from the seawater, Riva 1920 can give it new life as a functional work of art.

The company's process could not stand in more direct contrast to that of the vast majority of its competitors. Today, even most high-end wooden furniture is made with some particle board: wood chips, shavings, and saw dust mixed with a resin and pressed into shape. To create the illusion of solid wood throughout, the particle board is covered with a thin layer of real wood. Who would know the difference?

Illusions play a role even in the typical claim of reforested wood. Some countries don't follow the rules. It takes skillful detective work to ensure that so-called reforested wood has met all the requirements of that certification. This is something Riva 1920 is more than willing to do. As much as the company loves its traditions, it also recognizes that everything about the way it makes its furniture is necessarily temporary. In a decade, many of the materials it uses today may no longer be available from sustainable sources. It is the spirit of the company that must be sustained. The methods will adapt to a changing environment.

The Italian preoccupation with authenticity is inextricably tied with ideas of sustainability, history, and heritage. In my discussions with Maurizio Riva, he made clear that his most important job as CEO is to hand the fourth generation of the family the reins of a company as strong as the one whose reins were handed to him. Not only commercially successful, but as exciting and relevant as it was when he took over. This attitude affects all his behaviors as CEO. Every morning on his way to work, Maurizio collects any paper litter along the path into the factory and recycles it. His obsession with sustaining the company into the future is matched only by his reverence for its past.

Why is all of this important? Because surprise requires a willingness to take risks. Not only risks to the company but to the individuals within it. You have to be willing to put your neck on the line if you're going to surprise your customers instead of merely meeting market expectations. This requires a commitment to excellence that begins at the top of the organization. Employees must feel certain that they have the support of leadership when going above and beyond. For the employees themselves, risk requires pride, passion, and a sense of ownership. Family-owned businesses have an advantage in this department, which is why these are the companies that so often achieve and maintain disruptive quality, decade after decade.

THE FUTURE OF SURPRISE

Riva 1920 takes human resources as seriously as its natural ones. As I discovered on my own visit, the company serves gelato to all employees on hot days. This put me in mind of one of my first jobs, working for a liquor company when I was nineteen. Every morning, a pair of employees would visit each department to serve each worker a complimentary shot of brandy. (At illy, we stop short of that, but employees are entitled to a coffee or tea.)

This concern for the well-being of its workers extends to every corner of the operation. Working with heavy equipment is inherently dangerous, so the company spares no expense in ensuring the safety of its employees. This idea of a family business extends to every Riva worker. Each machine is equipped with state-of-the-art safeguards to prevent injuries that were once common in manufacturing. These devices are very expensive, and not all of them are required by current regulations. Many manufacturers in the United States, for example, still use machines that don't automatically deactivate if a finger brushes against a saw, even though the technology for this is available. (Something tells me that these CEOs would pay for the upgrade if their own family members were holding those planks in their bare hands.)

Riva 1920 invests not only in its own employees but in the community at large. It hosts an annual contest for young designers. It teaches recovering drug addicts how to work with wood to help them get back on their feet and then exhibits the results of their efforts with reclaimed wine casks in cities around the world as an inspiration to others struggling with addiction. It even runs an annual festival where it distributes small oak trees that can be planted in nearby parks or gardens.

In all of this, we see Riva 1920's commitment to the future, and this is so important to the discussion of surprise because, in order to be willing to take a risk on surprising customers, you must have the long view in mind. If your only concern is this quarter's performance, it will always make the most sense to play it safe and stick to the status quo. Surprise is an essential indicator of long-term thinking and it requires the sincere commitment and heartfelt passion of everyone in the company to make it happen.

INCANTO

Throughout this book we have talked often about the importance of making products of high quality. Yet there is another element to the equation, this one more the choice of the individual buying the product: quantity.

More is not always better. It is tempting to collect, to accrue, to add. And yes, we all have collections of things we are passionate about. For me it is small figurines of frogs. Many years ago I wrote a book called *La Rana Chinese* (The Chinese Frog). Ever since, my friends and acquaintances have made a habit of giving me small ceramic, glass, or metal frogs as gifts. Yet, life is not about attaining more; it is about attaining better, in sufficient quantity, with neither deficiency nor excess.

One of my favorite poets is Giacomo Leopardi. He wrote a poem, beloved to any Italian who has experienced rural life, called "Il Sabato Del Villaggio" (The Saturday of the Village). The poem describes the feelings of anticipation in a village the evening before the day of rest. The young girls are collecting ribbons and flowers for their hair. The young boys anticipate the feasting, and the old women reminisce about their youth and beauty. The village is enthralled in the feeling of

expectation for the next day's joy, even as the poem acknowl-
edges that it is only a short reprieve from their week's labor:

Be happy little lad;
a joyful time is this.
More I'd not tell you, but if your holiday
seems somewhat tardy yet, let not that grieve you.

This poem is beloved because it speaks to a central truth.
Anticipation and nostalgia are wrapped into one. Even as we
look forward to something, we are already mourning the
fleetingness of the experience. Every real joy in life is tran-
sient. A first kiss is mingled with the last in our minds. A
sunny day is filled with bittersweet joy because we know eventually it will rain.

I have let this awareness steer me through life. I own good
things, but not too many of them. I eat good food, but not
too much of it. I never eat or enjoy so much of something
that I completely satiate my desire for it; I always stop eating
a few bites short of being completely full. I never want to
drink so much wine (and endure the resulting hangover)
that I don't anticipate another glass with pleasure.

The joys of life that are most profound are the simplest.
The small things with a great quality, that almost everyone
can afford daily, are the ones that can fill our life with satisfaction. This, then, is your opportunity. When you begin a
new business, you have two possibilities: you can invent something new, or you can dramatically improve a product that
already exists. Incanto is a way of infusing those products with
that extra element of surprise and delight. It is about pursuing augmented perfection or refining what you do to the
point where your competitors cannot hope to copy it. It is
about taking your time and building fewer things, better. It is

about cultivating a sense of family both with your employees and your customers. And it is about bringing a very Italian sense of beauty to all that you do.

It makes sense that I have dedicated my life to making simple things very very well. Because I believe that this is where the great pleasures of Incanto are found.

ACKNOWLEDGMENTS

A special thanks to Marco Mari and Carlotta Borruto, Caroline Greeven, Myra Fiori, and the managers of all the companies I visited and interviewed that are cited in the book.

NOTES

CHAPTER ONE

1. Natalie Kitroeff and David Gelles, "Claims of Shoddy Production Draw Scrutiny to a Second Boeing Jet," *New York Times*, April 20, 2019, https://www.nytimes.com/2019/04/20/business/boeing -dreamliner-production-problems.html.
2. After a Boeing whistleblower made these claims, Boeing pushed back against *New York Times'* reporting, and Qatar issued a press release denying problems.
3. However, as there is no evidence the playwright actually visited Italy, I advise caution if a local claims to be able to guide you to the locations featured in the play (this is doubly true if you visit Verona, the setting for *Romeo and Juliet*, and a guide offers to take you to Juliet's balcony).
4. Franz Lidz, "At the Sourdough Library, with Some Very Old Mothers," *New York Times*, April 11, 2020, https://www.nytimes.com/2020 /04/11/science/sourdough-bread-starter-library.html.
5. Panettone is a bread rich with eggs, butter, and fruit, traditionally eaten around Christmas, though it is becoming more of a year-round delicacy.

CHAPTER TWO

1. Guglielmo Mattioli, "What Caused the Genoa Bridge Collapse—and the End of an Italian National Myth?" *Guardian*, February 26, 2019,

https://www.theguardian.com/cities/2019/feb/26/what-caused
-the-genoa-morandi-bridge-collapse-and-the-end-of-an-italian-national
-myth.

2. David Segal and Gaia Pianigiani, "Genoa Bridge Collapse Throws
   Harsh Light on Benettons' Highway Billions," *New York Times*, March
   5, 2019, https://www.nytimes.com/2019/03/05/world/europe
   /genoa-bridge-italy-autostrade-benetton.html.

3. Mindi Chahal, "How Benetton Is Changing Its Colours," *Marketing
   Week*, December 2, 2015, https://www.marketingweek.com/benetton
   -changes-its-colours/.

4. "Benetton's Italian Founder Returns to Save Company, Age 82,"
   Local, November 30, 2017, https://www.thelocal.it/20171130/luciano
   -benetton-founder-return.

5. Read Jack Trout's classic *Positioning: The Battle for Your Mind*
   (McGraw-Hill Education, January 3, 2000) for more on this.

CHAPTER THREE

1. Don Norman's *Emotional Design* (Basic Books, 2005) is a good place
   to start if you want to learn more about this theory.

CHAPTER FOUR

1. Pilita Clark, "Family Businesses Are Welcome Winners in the Pandemic," *Financial Times*, January 23, 2021, https://www.ft.com/content
   /acb9d0c3-bbfc-471d-9d66-9c37d482ab1f.

2. Eli Rosenberg, "Walmart and McDonald's Have the Most Workers on
   Food Stamps and Medicaid, New Study Shows," *Washington Post*, November 18, 2020, https://www.washingtonpost.com/business/2020
   /11/18/food-stamps-medicaid-mcdonalds-walmart-bernie-sanders/.

3. Su-San Sit, "Wal-Mart Squeezes Suppliers in Price War," *Supply Management* (Chartered Institute of Procurement & Supply), March 31,
   2017, https://www.cips.org/supply-management/news/2017
   /march/wal-mart-to-squeeze-suppliers-to-win-discount-chain-price
   -war-/.

CHAPTER FIVE

1. Eugenia Scabini, "Parent-Child Relationships in Italian Families:
   Connectedness and Autonomy in the Transition to Adulthood," *Psi-

cologia: Teoria e Pesquisa 16, no. 1 (April 2000), 23–30, https://doi
.org/10.1590/S0102-37722000000100004.

2. Jeannie Marshall, "Italy's Stay-at-Home Kids," *Maclean's*, April 24,
   2014, https://www.macleans.ca/society/life/stay-at-home-kids/.

CHAPTER SEVEN

1. Liberate Project, "What Is Vanilla and Where Does It Come From?"
   November 9, 2020, https://www.liberate-project.eu/what-is
   -vanillin-and-where-does-it-come-from/.
2. Nils-Gerrit Wunsch, "On Average, How Often Do You Eat Pasta?"
   Statista, November 24, 2020, https://www.statista.com/statistics
   /730668/frequency-of-eating-pasta-in-italy/.
3. B. Liu, S. Asseng, C. Müller, et al, "Similar Estimates of Temperature
   Impacts on Global Wheat Yield by Three Independent Methods,"
   Nature Climate Change 6 (2016), 1130–1136, https://doi.org/10.1038
   /nclimate3115, https://www.nature.com/articles/nclimate3115.

CHAPTER EIGHT

1. Simon J. Woolf, "Vodopivec, A Perfect Expression of Vitovska," The
   Morning Claret, July 15, 2018, https://www.themorningclaret
   .com/2018/vodopivec-a-perfect-expression-of-vitovska/.
2. Margherita, "Bitto Cheese & the Disappearing Traditions of Valgerola,"
   The Crowded Planet, April 4, 2016, https://www.thecrowdedplanet
   .com/bitto-cheese-valgerola/.
3. A DOP certification requires a recipe, and the group insisted the Bitto
   producers supply one, leading to a rare backlash against the certificate
   and the certification process. Now there are multigenerational Bitto
   producers who are unable to call their cheese by its name.
4. Andrew Wheeler, "Everything You Need to Know About Balsamic Vinegar," Serious Eats, August 10, 2018, https://www.seriouseats.com
   /everything-you-need-to-know-guide-to-balsamic-vinegar.
5. "Balsamic Vinegar, the Nectar of Modena, Italy," Walks of Italy, June 17,
   2011, https://www.walksofitaly.com/blog/food-and-wine/balsamic
   -vinegar-modena-italy.
6. "5 Things You May Not Know About San Marzano Tomatoes," Food
   Republic, July 8, 2014, https://www.foodrepublic.com/2014/07
   /08/5-things-you-might-not-know-about-san-marzano-tomatoes/.

CHAPTER NINE

1. Aditya Chakrabortty, "Why Doesn't Britain Make Things Anymore?" *Guardian*, November 16, 2011, https://www.theguardian.com/business/2011/nov/16/why-britain-doesnt-make-things-manufacturing.
2. Jacob Morgan, "Why Every Employee Should Be Building Weak Ties at Work," *Forbes*, March 11, 2014, https://www.forbes.com/sites/jacobmorgan/2014/03/11/every-employee-weak-ties-work/?sh=4c842d993168.
3. Philip Sopher, "Where the Five-Day Workweek Came From," *Atlantic*, August 21, 2014, https://www.theatlantic.com/business/archive/2014/08/where-the-five-day-workweek-came-from/378870/.

CHAPTER TEN

1. Matthew Yglesias, "Southern Europe's Small-Business Problem," *Slate*, July 6, 2012, https://slate.com/business/2012/07/the-small-business-problem-why-greece-italy-and-spain-have-too-many-small-firms.html.
2. Adam Satariano and Emma Buboia, "Pasta, Wine and Inflatable Pools: How Amazon Conquered Italy in the Pandemic," *New York Times*, September 26, 2020, https://www.nytimes.com/2020/09/26/technology/amazon-coronavirus-pandemic.html.
3. Isobel Asher Hamilton and Qayyah Moynihan, "Amazon Warehouse Workers Striking in Outrage at the Firm's Response to 2 Staff Contracting Coronavirus," *Business Insider*, March 17, 2020, https://www.businessinsider.com/amazon-workers-strike-coronavirus-2020-3.
4. Hannah Roberts and Giorgio Leali, "Alitalia: Too Italian to Fail," *Politico*, May 28, 2020, https://www.politico.eu/article/alitalia-airline-too-italian-to-fail/.
5. Francesca Landini, "UPDATE 1—New, State-Owned Alitalia May Replace Old Carrier in April—CEO," *Reuters*, December 9, 2020, https://www.reuters.com/article/alitalia-strategy/update-1-new-state-owned-alitalia-may-replace-old-carrier-in-april-ceo-idUSL8N2IP59K.
6. A specifically Italian style of operatic singing, with precise and agile control over the vocals. It fell out of fashion as "heavier" and more dramatic operatic singing came into vogue in the early 1900s. Now, however, there is a revival of the operas of Bellini and Donizetti, specifically well suited to the style.

7. Glen Barkman, "A Few Words with Paolo Fazioli," Piano Price Point, https://pianopricepoint.com/fazioli-piano-information/.

CHAPTER ELEVEN

1. Theodore Levitt, "Marketing Success Through Differentiation—of Anything," *Harvard Business Review,* January 1, 1980, https://hbr.org/1980/01/marketing-success-through-differentiation-of-anything.
2. In *Competitive Advantage,* Michael Porter, a professor at Harvard Business School, argued that, to perfectly satisfy the needs of the most demanding customers, companies must tailor their goods to a "segment of one."

INDEX

ABOUT THE AUTHOR

RICCARDO ILLY is an entrepreneur in the superpremium food sector.

Chairman of Polo del Gusto, he has always been in search of the ultimate quality and uniqueness for the consumer.

Starting from the 1990s, Illy embarked on a political career, becoming mayor of Trieste, deputy of the Italian Parliament, and president of the autonomous region Friuli-Venezia Giulia, as well as president of the Assembly of European Regions.

He is a freelance journalist and the author of several books.

Since 2018, he has been leading a course on Disruptive Quality.

Illy was appointed as Royal Warrant Holder by the UK Royal House.

He was conferred the title of Grande Ufficiale by the president of the Italian Republic and the Grand Decoration of Honour in Gold by the president of the Austrian Republic.

He is Honorary Consul of the French Republic in Trieste.

Born in 1955, he is married and has a daughter.